Support for Principals

Support for Principals

Firsthand Experiences in Planning Programs and Activities

Edited by Lee A. Westberry

ROWMAN & LITTLEFIELD
Lanham • Boulder • New York • London

Published by Rowman & Littlefield
An imprint of The Rowman & Littlefield Publishing Group, Inc.
4501 Forbes Boulevard, Suite 200, Lanham, Maryland 20706
www.rowman.com

86–90 Paul Street, London EC2A 4NE

Copyright © 2022 by Lee A. Westberry

All rights reserved. No part of this book may be reproduced in any form or by any electronic or mechanical means, including information storage and retrieval systems, without written permission from the publisher, except by a reviewer who may quote passages in a review.

British Library Cataloguing in Publication Information Available

Library of Congress Cataloging-in-Publication Data

Names: Westberry, Lee A., 1969- editor.
Title: Support for principals : firsthand experiences in planning programs and activities / edited by Lee A. Westberry.
Description: Lanham : Rowman & Littlefield, [2022] | Includes bibliographical references. | Summary: "Support for Principals is a compilation of supporting professional development for principals"—Provided by publisher.
Identifiers: LCCN 2022015154 (print) | LCCN 2022015155 (ebook) | ISBN 9781475865622 (cloth) | ISBN 9781475865639 (paperback) | ISBN 9781475865646 (epub)
Subjects: LCSH: School principals—In-service training—United States. | Educational leadership—United States. | School management and organization—United States.
Classification: LCC LB1738.5 .S86 2022 (print) | LCC LB1738.5 (ebook) | DDC 371.2/012—dc23/eng/20220524
LC record available at https://lccn.loc.gov/2022015154
LC ebook record available at https://lccn.loc.gov/2022015155

I would like to dedicate this book to my mother, who has always been my biggest cheerleader. Her unwavering support has been the bedrock to my success.

Contents

Preface ix

Acknowledgments xi

Introduction xiii

1 Social and Emotional Needs of Principals 1
  Larry G. Daniel and Kevin Badgett, University of Texas Permian Basin

2 Systems Planning: An Essential Skill 15
  Lee Westberry, The Citadel

3 Action Research: A Powerful Tool for School Improvement 33
  Gail Gilmore, Renée N. Jefferson, and Lee Westberry, The Citadel

4 Technology Integration: Administrators Leading the Charge 53
  Rachel Biritz, Clemson University

5 The Importance of School Law for the School Leader 69
  Kent Murray, The Citadel

6 Principals and Special Education: What's the Big IDEA 87
  Amanda Stefanski, Christine LeBlanc, and Brennan Davis, Columbia College

7 Instructional Supervision: Supporting a Culture of Teaching
   and Learning 107
   Christine LeBlanc and Brennan Davis, Columbia College

8 From Having All the Answers to Engaging in Collective Learning:
   Reenvisioning the Role of the Principal and the Approach
   to Support 125
   *Paula Tharp, Myron B. Labat, and Leigh A. McMullan,
   Mississippi State University*

About the Editor and Contributors 143

Preface

Principals are the gatekeepers who hold the keys to the kingdom otherwise known as school. They are responsible for establishing a clear vision for education, a mission for all educators, and strategies that will make the vision a reality. This is a massive undertaking considering the plethora of leadership and management tasks that must be planned, not to mention the tasks that surface daily and sometimes minute by minute. Being an effective school principal is not for the faint at heart.

Not only is the principal the leader of a school, but they're also a leading light in the community. Parents and businesses alike have great expectations for the principal to not only provide a challenging and safe school environment but also bolster the local employment trends. In essence, the responsibilities that a principal shoulders are substantial. Because of the importance of the position and the changing demands of society, principals must stay abreast of current job market trends, legal cases, technological innovations, school improvement research, and the like. In order to remain current and relevant, districts must provide a system of principal support. This book will outline many areas of continued support needed for today's principals in the hopes that districts will provide the assistance needed and that principals will take charge to lead their own learning efforts.

Dr. Lee A. Westberry
Editor

Acknowledgments

I would like to acknowledge all the principals who work so tirelessly to serve our children. As a former principal and a parent, I understand your plight. Know you are appreciated. I would also like to acknowledge the contributors to this volume. Their work serves administrators all over the world.

Introduction

Support for Principals: Firsthand Experiences in Planning Programs and Activities is a compilation of research from practitioners and professionals across the nation. Each chapter is designed to provide insight into the support needed for principals and how to achieve that support. Topics were selected based on the principals' feedback as to the support they most need today to operate effectively.

Knowing that "sit and get" meetings are not the best method of support, each chapter highlights a "how to" approach for district leaders to consider. The insight shared is derived from years of experience in the field as either a participant in the support or the organizer of that support. Additionally, each chapter includes a summary and reflection questions for further thought and inquiry.

The contributors' biographical information is included at the end of the book so that the readers may contact them for additional information or support needed. The journey to continue to improve our schools is not a singular or lonely one, as resources are available.

Chapter One

Social and Emotional Needs of Principals

Larry G. Daniel and Kevin Badgett,
University of Texas Permian Basin

Even the casual reader of literature on educational practice in the past three decades has noticed articles on the topic of social-emotional learning (SEL) in schools. Indeed, SEL has taken education by storm, and the prevailing opinion among twenty-first-century educators is that SEL is both "foundational and essential" (Stefanovic, Reyes-Guerra, & Zorovich-Godek, 2021, p. 59) to the learning environment of the school. As Mahoney, Durlak, and Weissberg (2019) note, "Social and emotional learning . . . is critical to students' long-term success in and out of school, and it merits careful, sustained attention throughout K-12 education" (p. 18).

Some have argued (e.g., Stefanovic et al., 2021) that SEL is actually a return to a set of standard educational practices that were typical of education in the first half of the twentieth century prior to the rise of standardized testing. Indeed, educators prepared some years ago will recall a focus on building educational goals and objectives in both the affective and the cognitive domain. SEL has in many ways brought the affective domain back to learning and the practice of schooling.

The rise of importance of SEL has created demands for school principals both to have a broad understanding of SEL and to be able to direct teachers and other school personnel to implement effective SEL programs (Mahfouz, Greenberg, & Rodriguez, 2019; Schlund, 2021). However, SEL has not typically been stressed in principal preparation programs nor has the principal's role as a leader in SEL implementation been adequately explored. In fact, Mahfouz (2018) lamented that districts implementing SEL focus on teachers, curricula, and standards, but too often overlook the importance of the principal's role in implementation of SEL.

SEL is also directly and personally relevant to the principal. Principals must be aware of their own social-emotional needs and competencies

(Cherniss, 1998; Patti et al., 2018). In order to stay emotionally healthy and keep up with the demands of their jobs, "principals must acquire effective skills and strategies to deal with stress and support their mental health and well-being" (Greenberg et al., 2019, p. 18).

PURPOSE

It is the purpose of this chapter to provide an overview of SEL with emphasis on what principals need to know both to lead SEL efforts and to be sensitive of their own needs in the social-emotional domain. Ideas are divided into three categories: (1) an overview of SEL and its rise in education, (2) a discussion on the knowledge and skills that principals and other building-level school leaders need to effectively lead SEL efforts in their schools, and (3) the presentation of strategies useful for addressing principals' specific social and emotional needs. Finally, a set of reflection questions is proffered for school administrators focused on their own SEL needs.

A CURSORY OVERVIEW OF SEL

In recent years, schools in the United States and across the globe have become heavily focused on the social and emotional needs of students, resulting in the development of curricula, teaching strategies, and educational outcomes related to SEL. A prime motivator in the popularity of SEL was the development in 1994 of the Collaborative for Academic, Social, and Emotional Learning (CASEL, n.d.), a nonprofit organization devoted to the development of social and emotional learning in children and adults.

CASEL (n.d.) defines SEL as

> the process through which all young people and adults acquire and apply the knowledge, skills, and attitudes to develop healthy identities, manage emotions and achieve personal and collective goals, feel and show empathy for others, establish and maintain supportive relationships, and make responsible and caring decisions. (para. 1)

In recent years, the education profession has widely recognized the importance of SEL and its role in addressing the well-being of children. Many children experience trauma early in life and/or live in unstable environments that impact their emotional well-being. Aviles, Anderson, and Davila (2006) note, in particular, that children and adolescents who have been exposed to violence manifest a range of emotional problems diminishing their development of social and emotional competencies. These issues may cause adjustment issues, lead to emotional or violent outbursts, and hamper ability for academic success.

SEL advocates have argued that students who are emotionally well balanced and have strong relationships with others will be more successful in school. Darling-Hammond (2019), for example, describes SEL as an educational "missing link" (para. 5) vitally important in helping students understand themselves and others and connected to important outcomes such as self-understanding, social skill development, student learning growth, and school safety. Moreover, Schlund (2021) astutely observed that educators have increasingly recognized the importance of SEL as schools have responded to the COVID-19 pandemic.

The goal of SEL is to promote social and emotional competence in children. As Elias et al. (1997, p. 2) note:

> Social and emotional competence is the ability to understand, manage, and express the social and emotional aspects of one's life in ways that enable the successful management of life tasks such as learning, forming relationships, solving everyday problems and adapting to the complex demands of growth and development. It includes self-awareness, control of impulsivity, working cooperatively and caring about oneself and others.

SEL has grown in popularity and has been implemented in schools, despite obstacles such as insufficient professional development, lack of funding, and competition with other educational priorities (Schlund, 2021). Although parents have expressed concern about some specific SEL activities, they are generally supportive of related efforts. Nevertheless, few would argue against the importance of building students' emotional fortitude and their ability to engage socially in meaningful and positive ways. The popularity of SEL is also fueled by a common belief that students who are socially and emotionally well-adjusted will perform better in school.

To test the perceived SEL-learning link, researchers have begun to explore the relationship between SEL and achievement, and the overwhelming evidence suggests a positive correlation. Among those noteworthy effects, SEL consistently contributed positively to reading and math achievement, standardized test scores, course grades, and teachers' informal reports of student performance.

SEL advocates suggest that, in addition to its possible positive effects on student achievement, SEL may also help to advance a range of desirable social outcomes. For example, Berman (2021) made a case for using SEL activities as a tool for promoting goals related to diversity, equity, and inclusion, considering that SEL allows students to better understand their own feelings as well as the perspectives of others.

Berman (2021) concluded that "social-emotional learning ensures students experience culturally inclusive and identify-safe classrooms that promote a sense of belonging" (p. 8). Likewise, Darling-Hammond (2019) provided evidence that SEL may also be beneficial in addressing school discipline problems. When schools engage students in SEL activities, such as self-reflection, anger management, teacher-student advisory pairings, and instruction about positive peer relationships, discipline improves and schools become safer environments that more effectively foster learning.

PRINCIPAL KNOWLEDGE AND SKILLS FOR LEADING SEL

As building-level administrators, principals are responsible for creating a culture that supports SEL and for ensuring that aspects of the curriculum devoted to development of SEL are appropriately implemented (Mahfouz et al., 2019). Principals must also assure that the culture of the school protects the social and emotional needs of faculty and staff such that workplace bullying and other deleterious behaviors do not manifest themselves in the educational workplace (Fahie & Devine, 2014). As Mahfouz (2018) notes, "A healthy, positive school culture is created by leaders with emotional stability" (p. 602).

Over the past decade, an extensive literature base has developed on the role of principals in assuring implementation of SEL for students (e.g., Beatty & Campbell-Evans, 2020; Carstarphen & Graff, 2018; Schlund, 2021). In a qualitative study focused on principals' perceived roles and responsibilities for ensuring development of a culture to support SEL, Beatty and Campbell-Evans (2020) found that principals placed SEL as a high priority in their schools, viewing it as a key ingredient for assuring a culture of student learning and engagement.

In this same vein, Mahfouz et al. (2019) note that principals with strong social-emotional competence are more likely to create a welcoming atmosphere for students and their families. Principals' emotional and social competence is linked to outcomes such as effective leadership, healthy relationships, effective community relations, and effective implementation of SEL in schools (Greenberg et al., 2019).

Mahfouz et al. (2019) proposed a "prosocial school leader" model focused on linkages between the principal's own social and emotional competence and his or her ability to demonstrate the characteristics needed for assuring that teachers, students, staff, and parents feel safe, cared for, and valued.

These effective leadership characteristics lead to a healthy school climate and positive social and academic outcomes.

The social-emotional competence of the principal is the key to the development of a culture to maximize SEL: "Principals lay the foundations for positive relationships among stakeholders of the schools, especially those relations among students, teachers, and the community" (Mahfouz et al., 2019, p. 4). Consequently, it is becoming incumbent upon contemporary preservice programs for preparing principals and school district in-service programs for school leaders to ensure that the principals have a broad understanding of SEL.

Principals need to inculcate a knowledge of ways to incorporate SEL into the school curriculum, build SEL into the school culture, and model emotional intelligence to others within the school building (Mahfouz et al., 2019). A review of the literature includes a variety of strategies for advancing principals' skill base in becoming leaders for SEL, whether in a principal preparation program or via district-based professional development:

1. *Focus on Developing Emotional Intelligence.* In an interview with Daniel Goleman, a leading emotional intelligence scholar, Vitale (2021) explored the concept of emotional balance in the life of the educational leader. It is important that school leaders openly express positive emotions that can build enthusiasm and motivate teachers and students.

    Put another way, "Emotional intelligence is good for business" (Stefanovic et al., 2012, p. 58). Principals can build a foundation for SEL by creating an expectation that emotions matter and that expressing positive emotions can set the tone for a positive learning environment (Patti et al., 2018). Principals should model effective expression of emotions and their impact on quality of experiences in the school environment.

2. *Embed SEL within the Larger Concept of Transformative Leadership.* Stefanovic et al. (2021) described a course in leadership for SEL developed at Florida Atlantic University. The experiences of the instructors with a cohort of leadership candidates are presented. Transformative leadership served as the foundation on which the course was structured.

    Transformative leaders view themselves as leaders of social change with a focus on elevating the lives of students, their families, and their communities. This is in contrast to transactional leadership, which focuses on the immediate actions the principal should take in order to have students and teachers engage in appropriate behaviors. Transformative leaders focus on the school's vision and not just the immediate outcomes desired.

3. *Include Peer Coaching.* In their principal preparation pilot study, Stefanovic et al. (2021) rotated peer coaches across the students in the cohort.

Peers reviewed one another's strategies for fostering students' voices, agency, and engagement in the school environment. Likewise, Carstarphen and Graff (2018) spoke about the value of their experiences in a peer learning community as part of a national cohort of school districts implementing SEL.

Mahfouz et al. (2019) also identified the value of peer coaching and mentoring but were quick to note that there is no research to support the effectiveness of these strategies in increasing SEL in school leaders. Obviously, more research is needed, but few would deny the intuitive link between peer coaching activities and eventual principal performance.

4. *Focus on Alignment across School Activities.* Effective professional development for SEL helps the principal to see connections among the school or district's SEL policies, strategies employed by the school to promote student well-being, and the specific SEL program or activities employed on students. For example, an SEL curriculum that focuses on the students' voice in devising and implementing their own solutions to problems may not thrive in the midst of an authoritative discipline program (Schlund, 2021).

5. *Focus on the Link between School Culture and Learning.* In a qualitative study focused on the approaches school leaders take in developing a culture focused on learning, Beatty and Campbell-Evans (2020) found that school leaders placed a high priority on the social and emotional development of their students. Learning was appropriately viewed by the participants as the most important outcome of the school, and SEL was viewed as the primary means for developing a positive culture to support learning.

    A lack of attentiveness to SEL may actually deter student achievement. As Stefanovic et al. (2021) note, "An imbalanced leadership approach focusing on achievement alone diminishes the power of the school leaders' influence to inspire and support staff and students" (p. 61). By contrast, an emotionally intelligent leader has the ability to build motivation among teachers and students leading to a high level of achievement.

6. *Focus on Relationships.* The ability to engage positively with others is one facet of emotional intelligence (Cherniss, 1998). Students learn best when they know that their teacher and leaders value them as people and get to know them as individuals. Supportive relationships are the foundation upon which the school builds SEL. School leaders in Beatty and Campbell-Evans's (2020) study focused on "developing strong, supportive relationships between teachers and students" (p. 443) which led to "well-adjusted students who are able to engage in learning" (p. 445).

    In short, SEL is enhanced when the principal and teachers in the school model positive relationships and when the culture formed as a result of these positive relationships results in an enhanced learning environment.

Mahfouz et al. (2019) stressed the importance of principals promoting an "ethic of care," "listening with full attention," and "approaching decision making with an open and accepting attitude" (pp. 4–5) as key components of creating a caring environment in which SEL thrives.

7. *Promote School Leaders' Self-Awareness.* Educators can most effectively implement SEL when they are self-aware. In their pilot study to promote effective leadership for SEL, Stefanovic et al. (2021) used findings from neuroscience to help their principal candidates understand how the brain works when individuals are exposed to various stressful situations.

"Brain science" activities, such as the ones employed by Stefanovic et al., can lead to a better understanding of the impact of emotions on cognitive processing, promoting principals' awareness of the impact of their own emotions. The activities can also help principals, in turn, develop new ways to help students understand the impact of emotions on their decision-making.

ADDRESSING PRINCIPALS' SOCIAL AND EMOTIONAL NEEDS

School leadership is multifaceted and challenging. Among the many tasks of the principal is the responsibility for cultivating a positive learning environment and a shared sensitivity to the social-emotional context in which students learn, grow, and strive. Hence, the principal's own psychological well-being and emotional intelligence are of paramount importance. Unfortunately, principals experience considerable job-related stress, the risk of eventual burnout is high (DeMatthews et al., 2021), and there is a particularly high likelihood of work-related stress for new principals (Sackstein, 2018).

Mahfouz et al. (2019) noted that the stress of the job may also create strain in relationships with stakeholders. In one study, principals experienced greater levels of stress even as support from the community increased (Beausaert et al., 2016). Principal turnover rates are becoming increasingly higher, and principals in schools in which a high percentage of students are from economically disadvantaged backgrounds have a 40 percent higher likelihood of turnover than their counterparts serving schools with greater percentages of nondisadvantaged students (Goldring & Taie, 2018).

High-stress occupations often get negative publicity. There is evidence that the perceived stresses of school leadership roles may be driving away good candidates from the work. For example, in a national survey of superintendents, Cooper, Fusarelli, and Carella (2000) found that participants were alarmed at the shortage of applicants for school executive positions as well as the quality of the applicants. Finding effective school leaders also means finding a correct balance of formal and "soft" skills. As Cherniss (1998) put it, "Astute administrators have long recognized that effective leadership depends as much on character as on cognition" (p. 26).

The pressures of leading a school often result in school leaders devoting an inordinate amount of attention to maintaining their own mental and physical health and struggling to maintain appropriate balance between their work and personal lives (Hawk, 2008; Kaefele, 2020/2021). This is particularly difficult for new principals who may find the transition from teacher to leader much more difficult than they had anticipated (Sackstein, 2018).

Beausaert et al. (2016) notes that burnout is a significant problem for principals in many countries across the world and that "the prevalence of burnout is higher in the educational sector than in other sectors" (p. 349). These and other factors related to stress, time management, and general emotional well-being should be proactively addressed as part of employee assistance services, in professional development for school leaders, and during the employee supervisory process.

Knowing that leaders will vary in their levels of emotional intelligence, it is important to build principals' capacity for creating empathetic school cultures (Berg & Oppong, 2020/2021). As a means for addressing these and other social-emotional needs of principals, a host of effective strategies has been proposed. Wellness-related principal professional development should focus on the following strategies as well as other related strategies:

1. *Coaching and Mentoring.* One-on-one coaching or mentoring and role-alike professional development learning communities are typically used to focus on technical aspects of the principal role, managerial skill development, and instructional supervision skills. These already-formed social relationships can provide the framework for peers identifying and assisting one another with social and emotional development needs (Mahfouz et al., 2019; Superville, 2021).

    DeMatthews et al. (2021) noted that peer support for the SEL needs of principals tends to form informally in the same way that peers incidentally assist one another with a host of tasks and activities related to effectiveness in the role of the principals. However, it would behoove school districts to more intentionally include these activities in their in-service professional development.

2. *Supervisory Assistance.* Principals' supervisors have the responsibility both to evaluate principal effectiveness and to provide assistance to afford principals the maximum opportunity for success. The supervisory/evaluation process can be a useful vehicle for addressing principals'

social-emotional needs. Affective components may be included as indicators on an evaluative instrument assessing the principal's emotional intelligence, and the supervisor may provide assistance and support via the role of critical friend or thought partner.

DeMatthews et al. (2021) dubbed this type of supervision as "self-care supervision" and noted that it was typically underutilized as a method for assisting school leaders with handling stress. Principals have a high regard for the opinions of their supervisors; hence, the role of the supervisor in identifying and assisting principals with stress cannot be overemphasized.

3. *Mindfulness Training.* Activities devoted to mindfulness (e.g., reflection, self-awareness, sensitivity to emotions and environment) have been found to correlate with positive outcomes related to improved self-care and better relationships in principals (Mahfouz, 2018; Mahfouz et al., 2019). Mahfouz et al. (2019) presented research findings to support positive outcomes of mindfulness practices. These outcomes included decreased stress, increased mental flexibility, and an ability to regulate emotions more effectively.

   Mindfulness is a powerful tool for positively shaping leader behavior. Brown and Olson (2015) discussed a range of strategies through which school leaders can practice mindfulness, including focused breathing, reflection, listening strategies, and visioning. Leader qualities cultivated through mindfulness include situational awareness, task attention, poise, and resilience (Murphy, 2011).

4. *Emotional Intelligence Training* (Mahfouz et al., 2021). It is generally believed that emotional intelligence is a set of skills that can be cultivated through training and practice. Various commercial programs are available for providing school leaders with training in emotional intelligence as well as activities principals can employ on a daily basis to build their "emotional quotient"—the ability to understand, evaluate, and express emotions effectively or, to "modulate emotions" (Cherniss, 1998, p. 27).

   However, school districts should use commercially available products with caution. Mahfouz et al. (2021) briefly mention several currently available commercial programs (e.g., Leading Schools with Heart and Mind, RULER SEL) for promoting emotional intelligence of school leaders but note there is unfortunately little to no research on the effectiveness of these programs.

   One study (Kearney, Kelsey, & Sinkfield, 2014) used a quasi-experimental design to study six interventions designed to increase the emotional intelligence of a cohort of principal program candidates at a university in Texas. Two of the interventions—active listening and time management—produced statistically significant differences, favoring the

intervention group, leading the researchers to advocate for continuance of emotional intelligence strategies in their principal preparation program.
5. *Wellness Activities* (Superville, 2021). School districts may implement a policy for principals taking wellness days during the school year or include specific activities to encourage administrators to focus on their wellness. In fact, school leaders often find that taking time off is one of the best ways to reduce stress and increase their own emotional well-being (Hawk, 2008).
6. *Making Multiyear Commitments to Principal Assignments* (Greenberg et al., 2019). It is common practice in many school districts to rotate principal assignments on a somewhat regular basis. Although this practice may be useful for a number of reasons or may be necessary if the district deems the principal is an inadequate "fit" for the school, longer assignments, whenever possible, provide principals stability that will both facilitate their own social and emotional development and create opportunities for deeper relationships with teachers, students, families, and other stakeholders.
7. *Self-Education.* Many resources to help individuals deal with stress and burnout and to help develop their social and emotional competence are available through self-help resources (DeMatthews et al., 2021). Although this is, on the surface, an individual strategy, school districts can facilitate self-education by making lists of resources and/or making resource libraries available to their principals.

SUMMARY

SEL has become an important component of school effectiveness. Leaders are expected to develop a positive school climate focused on strong relationships among all stakeholders. Leaders and teachers are charged with helping students learn strategies essential to developing healthy attitudes and habits to enable them to make good choices and achieve their goals in life. Though some principals are better equipped than others to build a culture to support SEL, emotional intelligence and prosocial behaviors can be developed in school leaders.

The strategies discussed herein are the strategies most commonly mentioned as effective for cultivating development of leaders' social and emotional competence. Admittedly, some of the identified strategies have a stronger research base to support them than others, but all of the identified strategies are supported by strong intuitive evidence. Although the efficacy of particular strategies may be debated, the importance of cultivating principals' capacity for leading SEL is clear.

The principal plays a vital role in improving school-based professional learning (Mahfouz, 2018), and the profession will benefit by focusing on SEL in principal preparation and in-service professional development. As with any educational initiative, SEL will only remain sustainable if there is leadership to support its continuance and advancement and if a culture is developed to support sustainability that is larger than any one leader. SEL has proven itself to be of sufficient value that it should not be in danger of extinction when leadership changes.

The COVID-19 pandemic, along with tension caused by diametrically opposed political ideologies, has resulted in emotional distress and social tension for many children and adolescents. Teachers and school leaders are also experiencing particularly high levels of stress. We trust, in this chapter, that we have drawn attention to the importance of mindfulness, emotional intelligence, and other strategies for principals both in dealing with job-related stress and in their development as leaders who can support the implementation of SEL.

REFLECTION QUESTIONS

1. To what extent do I understand the level of development of my own emotional intelligence? What tools can I use to assess my emotional intelligence? What professional development activities would allow me to enhance my emotional intelligence?
2. To what degree am I adequately addressing my home life/work balance? Am I engaging in wellness practices, self-care, and renewal essential to a proper mindset for leading SEL activities? What changes to my approach in the area of SEL might be warranted?
3. To what extent am I addressing my own emotional and psychological needs? What are some possible next steps to better understand and accommodate for my own emotional and psychological needs (e.g., Would I benefit from professional counseling and/or from developing closer connections with key professional friends who can assist me in developing leadership behaviors commensurate with emotional intelligence)?
4. To what degree am I engaging in transformational leadership? What can I do to better ensure that I keep in mind the larger goals of the school and how these goals impact the social-emotional development of my staff and students and not only focused on issues of the moment?

5. Is the culture of my school conducive to SEL? What steps have I taken to assess the culture? What actions can I take to ensure that our staff and students view SEL as a primary means for promoting a culture of learning?
6. Am I taking time to learn from other seasoned professionals? How can I be more purposeful and strategic in efforts connected to my own learning (e.g., Have I identified one or more coaches or mentors who can assist me in my social-emotional development and guide me in my leadership efforts related to SEL)?
7. What is the quality of my relationship with each of my staff members? Are there tensions that are preventing leadership team members or teachers at my school from feeling positive about their work and their ability to help students engage in SEL? If so, what options do I have to create a stronger culture in my school?
8. How well do I know my students? Do they have a relationship with me as the school's instructional leader? If my school is extremely large so that personal connections with all students are difficult, how can I assure that all the students are known by a member of our school's leadership team?
9. Do I practice mindfulness? To what extent do I constructively reflect on my behavior as a leader? What strategies could I use to practice sensitivity to the thoughts and feelings of others (staff, parents, students) in my school?
10. How can I better prepare myself to help my staff be more effective in SEL? (e.g., Am I regularly reading professional books, attending in-service activities on SEL, and assisting my teachers in developing curriculum and instructional approaches for addressing SEL?)

REFERENCES

Aviles, A. M., Anderson, T. R., & Davila, E. R. (2006). Child and adolescent social-emotional development with the context of school. *Child and Adolescent Mental Health*, *11*(1), 32–39.

Beatty, L., & Campbell-Evans, G. (2020). School leaders and a culture of support: Fostering student social emotional development. *Issues in Educational Research*, *30*(2), 435–51.

Beausaert, S., Forehlich, D. E., Devos, C., & Riley, P. (2016). Effects of support on stress and burnout in school principals. *Educational Research*, *58*(4), 347–65.

Berg, J. H., & Oppong, H. (2020/2021). Leading together: We're not OK, and that's OK. *Educational Leadership*, *78*(4), 80–81.

Berman, S. H. (2021). A path to equity paved by social-emotional learning. *School Administrator*, *78*, 8.

Brown, V., & Olson, K. (2015). *The mindful school leader: Practices to transform your leadership and school*. Thousand Oaks, CA: Corwin.

Carstarphen, M. J., & Graff, E. (2018). Seeding SEL across schools: Strategies for leaders. *Educational Leadership*, *76*(2), 30–34.

Cherniss, C. (1998). Social and emotional learning for leaders. *Educational Leadership*, *55*(7), 26–28.

Collaborative for Academic, Social, and Emotional Learning (CASEL). (n.d.). *Fundamentals of SEL*. Chicago, IL: Author. Retrieved from https://casel.org/fundamentals-of-sel/.

Cooper, B. S., Fusarelli, L. D., & Carella, V. A. (2000). *Career crisis in the superintendency: The results of a national study*. Arlington, VA: American Association of School Administrators.

Darling-Hammond, L. (2019). What makes social-emotional learning so important? *School Administrator*, *76*(7), 22–26.

DeMatthews, D., Carrola, P., Reyes, P., & Knight, D. (2021). School leadership burnout and job-related stress: Recommendations for district administrators and principals. *Clearing House*, *94*(4), 159–67.

Elias, M. J., Zins, J. E., Weissberg, R. P., Frey, K. S., Greenberg, M. T., Haynes, N. M., Kessler, R., Schwab-Stone, M. E., & Shriver, T. P. (1997). *Promoting social and emotional learning: Guidelines for educators*. Alexandria, VA: Association for Supervision and Curriculum Development.

Fahie, D., & Devine, D. (2014). The impact of workplace bullying on primary school teachers and principals. *Scandinavian Journal of Educational Research*, *58*(2), 235–52.

Goldring, R., & Taie, S. (2018). *Principal attrition and mobility: Results from the 2016–17 principal follow-up survey first look*. Washington, DC: U.S. Department of Education.

Greenberg, M. T., Mahfouz, J., Davis, M., & Turksma, C. (2019). Social emotional learning for principals: Strengthening leadership and well-being. *Education Canada*, *59*(4), 18–21.

Hawk, N. C. (2008). *Implications of stress and coping mechanisms in the superintendency* (Doctoral dissertation, University of Missouri-Columbia).

Kaefele, B. K. (2020/2021). The mental balancing act for school leaders. *Educational Leadership*, *78*(4), 50–54.

Kearney, W. S., Kelsey, C., & Sinkfield, C. (2014). Emotionally intelligent leadership: An analysis of targeted interventions for aspiring school leaders in Texas. *Planning and Changing*, *45*(1/2), 31–47.

Mahfouz, J. (2018). Mindfulness training for school administrators: Effects on well-being and leadership. *Journal of Educational Administration*, *56*(6), 602–19.

Mahfouz, J., Greenberg, M. T., & Rodriguez, A. (2019). *Principals' social and emotional competence: A key factor for creating caring schools* [Issue brief]. University Park, PA: Penn State College of Health and Human Development.

Mahoney, J. L., Durlak, J. A., & Weissberg, R. P. (2019). An update on social and emotional learning outcome research. *Phi Delta Kappan*, *100*(4), 18–23.

Murphy, J. T. (2011). Dancing in the rain: Tips on thriving as a leader in tough times. *Phi Delta Kappan, 93*(1), 36–41.

Patti, J., Holzer, A., Stern, R. S., Floman, J., & Brackett, M. A. (2018). Leading with emotional intelligence. *Educational Leadership, 75*(9), 46–51.

Sackstein, S. (2018). Going from teacher to leader—One educator's hard-earned tips on making the transition to an administrator role. *Educational Leadership, 75*(9), 64–69.

Schlund, J. (2021). SEL, equity and excellence: An expanded definition of social and emotional learning and what it means for school leaders. *Principal, 100*(5), 16–20.

Stefanovic, M., Reyes-Guerra, D., & Zorovich-Godek, D. (2021). SEL starts at the top. *The Learning Professional, 42*(1), 58–62.

Superville, D. R. (2021). Principals need social-emotional support, too. *Education Week, 41*(5), 19–21.

Vitale, J. (2021). The emotions of leadership: A conversation with Daniel Goleman. *School Administrator, 78*(9), 36.

Chapter Two

Systems Planning

An Essential Skill

Lee Westberry, The Citadel

WHAT IS A SYSTEM?

By anyone's definition, a system is a combination of things working together. Sounds simplistic, but it is not. In education, a system is an organized framework for operations. If administrators plan with an organized framework, then the work of administration becomes manageable. Systems provide a foundation and structure for the work of principals. "Without a system, principals are often left to continually put out fires and solve problems, never really undertaking the true task of instructional leadership" (Westberry, 2020, p. 1).

The increasing demands placed on principals and the heavy emphasis on instructional leadership demand that systems are developed in order to manage the position. Without these systems, principals have difficulty managing the demands, and the result is an increase in principal turnover rates (Fuller, 2012; Tyre, 2015). So, why is a systems approach not readily found in school administration? The answer may lie in the "how" rather than the "why." Too often, school administrators are told to do something without the knowledge of how to implement the program or idea.

To implement a system, one must think systemically. What will endure through time? What structures need to be in place to support the processes? What personnel are needed? Will the system operate with a change of personnel or in the principal's absence? One must consider each aspect of the work that is needed first. What is the outcome desired? From that point, the same backward by design planning must begin with thinking about the elements needed to obtain the desired effect. In doing so, one must consider how different aspects of the work of schools will impact other areas.

All systems are linked, and one must consider all systems needed in order to affect real change. See Figure 2.1, for an illustration of how systems

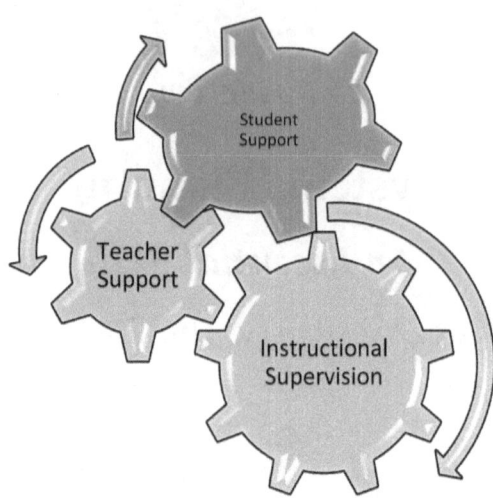

Figure 2.1. Systems Connections

connect to one another. In order to effectively provide instructional supervision and all that entails, there must be a strong system of teacher support and student support. Otherwise, instructional supervision can appear to be punitive and evaluative rather than supportive and developing.

Backward Planning the System

This author posits that there are four major systems to consider in school administration: curriculum and instruction, teacher support, student support, and culture (Westberry, 2020). Let us begin with one of the four major systems, curriculum and instruction, since there is such a heavy emphasis on this element today. What does curriculum and instruction mean? What are the elements needed in the system? One must first identify the elements before you can build a system.

Curriculum

With curriculum and instruction, one must begin with the curriculum itself. The definition of curriculum has certainly evolved over the years. Take a look at the following definitions of curriculum and note the differences:

- Douglas Reeves (2001)—An effective standards-based curriculum begins with desired results.
- James Popham (2003)—Curriculum is the representation of the educational ends.

- Peter Olivia (2005)—Curriculum is a number of plans, in written form and varying scope, that identify the desired learning experiences.
- Larry Ainsworth (2011)—In order to ensure that all students achieve the attainment of their course-specific standards, curriculum must be based on the alignment between standards, instruction, and assessment.

To begin, curriculum was defined by standards and expectations of student learning—the educational ends. Before standards, curriculum used to rely on a textbook. However, this definition has more recently evolved to include standards, instruction, and assessment. This definition should include resources as well. A developed curriculum should provide a strong foundation for teaching and learning. This is not to say that teachers are told how to teach, for that should remain in the purview of the experts—teachers.

However, the "what" to teach should be clearly defined with some of the needed resources to make a teacher's job easier. Of course, teachers are free to incorporate and utilize additional resources, but the curriculum should provide a starting point. Time is a resource that you can't renew, so saving teachers time in their planning should be considered useful, not limiting. Some teachers, however, find fault with a narrower curriculum (Crocco & Costigan, 2007), in that they feel it inhibits their creativity. The creativity is left to the teacher in how he or she teach the material, but assessing student progress is easier with a defined curriculum.

So, a curriculum system should include the standards, instruction, assessment, and resources. How this is provided and accessed by the teacher is a crucial part of the system. Most districts have some online platform or website in which teachers can access the curriculum. The question remains, however, if that curriculum is fully developed. If it is not, that is the first step in the process that needs to be addressed. Fill in the gaps.

Teachers can and will help define this curriculum if given the chance, and their input is integral to the success of any educational venture (Hopkins, Kroning, & Kobes, 2021; Mulenga & Mwanza, 2019). See Table 2.1, for an example of a developed portion of an English curriculum map that includes state standards, required instructional elements, concepts, cognitive levels of student learning, required resources, and additional resources. The missing element is the assessment or link to an assessment.

Why should the assessment be included? Including an assessment does not mean that all assessments for the unit should be included, such as all formative assessments. However, a common assessment is needed in order to analyze results and determine student mastery. Once the mapping is provided with materials and standards, the mapping must go one step further to ensure cognitive alignment of instruction and assessment.

Ainsworth (2011) states that a rigorous curriculum includes all elements that are intentionally cognitively aligned to the standards in order to guide instruction effectively. This means that curriculum must be mapped and aligned to the cognitive processes found in the standards, such as is found in the "skills" column in the table. However, teachers have to take this map one step further and break down the standards with supporting standards as well. This type of work can be done in their professional learning communities (PLCs).

Table 2.1. Developed Curriculum Map

EII-RL.5.1/EII-RI.5.1 cite strong and thorough textual evidence to support analysis of what the text says explicitly as well as inferences drawn from the text; identify multiple supported interpretations

Need to Know	Skills	What It Means	Required Resources	Additional Resources
Evidence Inference	Cite Identify	Cite evidence	A Shakespeare play such as *The Taming of the Shrew*, *Much Ado about Nothing*, *The Merchant of Venice* or *The Tragedy of Julius Caesar*	Close reading with JC https://www.folger.edu/close-reading-the-conspiracy-in-act-2 Folger Library www.folger.edu http://www.shakespeare-online.com https://www.tes.com/teaching-shakespeare/themes/

EII-RL.12.2 analyze how an author's choices concerning how to structure a text, order events within the text, and manipulate time to create different effects.

Events within the Text Manipulation of Time and Text Structure	Analyze	Determine significance of text structure and manipulation of time	Same as above or *Twelve Angry Men* by Reginald Rose	https://www.prestwickhouse.com/blog/post/2017/12/how-to-teach-twelve-angry-men http://www.samandscout.com/drama-and-persuasion-mini-unit-with-twelve-angry-men/ https://edsitement.neh.gov/launchpad-activities-twelve-angry-men

Source: Westberry (2020, p. 23).
Notes: Concepts: Central idea, claim, counterclaim, rebuttal, evidence, false statements, reasoning
Required Instructional Elements: Writing, Research, Close Reading

According to Dufour and Eaker (1998), teachers who work in PLCs serve as curriculum and instructional leaders as they work together to learn and grow in their profession in order to positively impact student achievement. Most teachers operate in some form of collaboration, so this is the perfect place to learn from each other's expertise. See Table 2.2, for a sample planning map for PLCs. More discussion about PLCs will come later in this chapter.

The elements of the planning map below break down the learning progressions for a standard and identify the key terms and mental processes needed in order to address the cognitive level of the standard. Mapping in this manner is important for teachers to understand how to plan instruction and assessment that is cognitively aligned. Misaligned instruction and assessment only set students up to fail when they are faced with high-stakes testing.

Table 2.2. Sample Planning Map

Standard 8.E.4: The student will demonstrate an understanding of the universe and the predictable patterns caused by Earth's movement in the solar system.

Supporting Standards	DOK Level	Key Terms
8.E.4B.1: Obtain and communicate information to model and compare the characteristics and movements of objects in the solar system (including planets, moons, asteroids, comets, and meteors).	DOK 2 Understand Apply DOK 4 Model Compare	Solar system, planets, moons, asteroids, comets, meteors, meteorite
8.E.4B.2: Construct explanations for how gravity affects the motion of objects in the solar system and tides on Earth.	DOK 2 Understand Construct	Gravity, neap tides, tilt, axis, day, year, elliptical, orbit
8.E.4B.4: Develop and use models to explain how motions within the Sun-Earth-Moon system cause Earth phenomena (including day and year, moon phases, solar and lunar eclipses, and tides).	DOK 2 Understand Model	Lunar movement, phases of the moon, eclipses, solar, lunar, tide
8.E.4B.6: Analyze and interpret data from the surface features of the Sun (including photosphere, corona, sunspots, prominences, and solar flares) to predict how these features may affect Earth.	DOK 4 Analyze Interpret	Photosphere, corona, sunspot, prominence, solar flares

Source: Westberry (2020, p. 23).

Elements of a Curriculum and Instruction System

Instructional Team

So, the elements of a developed curriculum and curriculum mapping have been revealed. How does an administrator devise a system to monitor and support this effort? One must start with the personnel and infrastructure that exists within a school. What does the instructional team look like? What are the strengths of the team? The organizational structure has a direct impact on the system that can be implemented.

Consider the administrative team and teacher leaders. How do they interact? What are their strengths and how can you organize duties in order to maximize benefit? All members of the team must report to the principal, as the principal should be involved and be the center for progress monitoring. For example, the use of department chairs and assistant principals may be ideal, or strong curriculum leaders within a department who are nominated for such a position may work with the administration. In either case, the team must be identified, and duties outlined. See Figure 2.2 for a sample team structure. This structure considers all roles available.

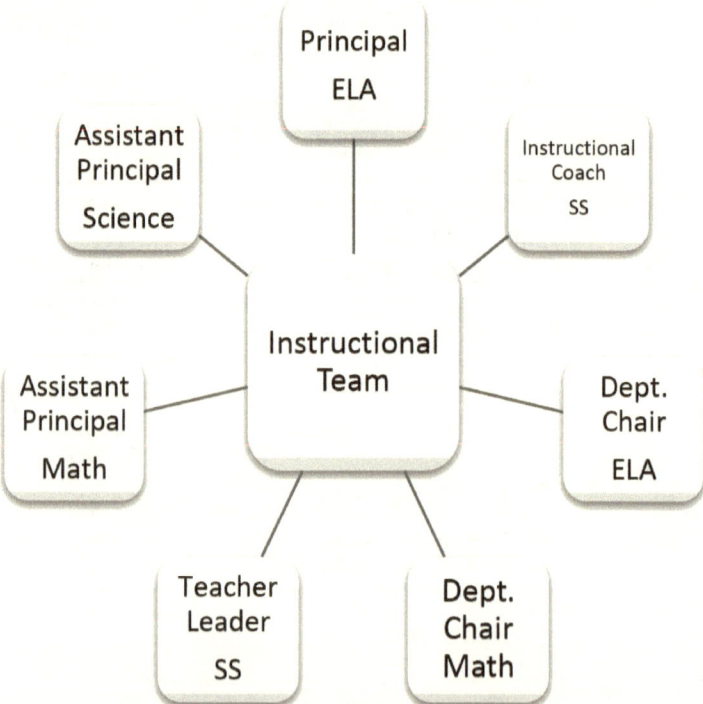

Figure 2.2. Sample Instructional Team Structure

Notice that the principal is not "above" or more important than any other team member, but the principal does work with all team members to support the instructional efforts of the school. Assistant principals need to be included in this team structure, as they need to learn instructional systems as well. The entire system is only as strong as the weakest link, and that is why each member needs to work collaboratively and not in isolation. A shared vision of the instructional system of the school will lead to cohesiveness and effectiveness.

If the district's curriculum maps include all the necessary elements, you can move straight to progress monitoring. If not, you start working with teachers and departments to fill in the missing elements to the maps you do have. With the understanding for the need for strong instructional maps, teachers will think more purposely about the materials and instruction they provide for the students.

Lesson Plans Now that the team is established, you must set up progress monitoring of the curriculum. How is this done? The first tool an administrator has at his or her disposal to assess curriculum is the lesson plans. Though lesson plans provide a roadmap of instruction for teachers, they also provide a roadmap of learning for administrators. Therefore, lesson plans must be an integral part of any curriculum and instruction system. Expectations for lesson plans must be explicit. For example, a principal must consider the following aspects of lesson plans:

1. What is the expected format?
2. What information is to be provided?
3. When are the lesson plans due to be turned in?
4. To whom do teachers turn in lesson plans?
5. What feedback is provided?
6. What form does the feedback take?
7. How is information from lesson plans used in curriculum and instruction systems planning?

Each of these questions must be answered with the instructional team before any expectations are made of the teaching faculty. The expectation should be that members of the instructional team share this responsibility, but the information gleaned from this experience is shared with the rest of the team. Teachers need to be trained on the lesson plan expectations and the system clearly outlined to them before you begin with a schoolwide expectation. Most importantly, though, teachers need to understand "why" this is the expectation.

Teachers, like most people, do not like exercises in futility. When teachers turn in lesson plans and no one reads them or provides any feedback, they often question the purpose. However, the purpose of lesson plans being turned in to the instructional team is to progress-monitor the curriculum so that strengths and weaknesses in the curriculum, planning, instruction, and assessment can be identified. This plan review helps to identify needed professional development as well as identify the experts in the building who can assist in that development.

Additionally, not all curricula are aligned perfectly to the standards and high-stakes testing expectations, and this type of review can help identify the gaps so that they can be filled. Patterns of behavior emerge from lesson plan review, and this information needs to be discussed among the instructional team in order to develop the appropriate teacher supports and the development of aligned curriculum units/materials. Without lesson plan review, administrators are left to rely on observations, and observations alone do not tell the story. See Table 2.3, for a sample lesson plan system of expectations and Figure 2.3 for a sample lesson plan critique form.

This type of system leaves no room for confusion. The lesson plan critique does have a direct correlation with the data to be gleaned. Smart administrators devise a form that provides some quantitative data to share. For example, a principal who can share that 80 percent of lesson plans for a two-week period were proficient in providing appropriate learning progressions but only 37 percent were proficient in providing checks for understanding, this message provides an area of opportunity for teachers to focus and for administrators to provide a focus for PLC's or professional development.

Table 2.3. Sample Lesson Plan Expectations

	Lesson Plans Expectations
Due Date	Fridays, the week prior to the week's lesson
Time	Due by 5:00 pm
Submission	Via email
Review	Review by Sunday evening at 8:00 pm
Reviewer	Assigned administration
English	Principal
Math	Instructional coach
Science	Designated AP
Social Studies	Designated AP
Feedback	Designated form
Discussion	Instructional team meetings
Monday Meeting	Rm. 257 @ 4:00 pm
Agenda and Minutes	Data shared with faculty

Lesson Plan Critique

Teacher _____   Date _____

Subject _____   Grade Level (s) _____

　　　　　　Lesson Plan Reviewer _____

Please use the scale below to rate the elements of the lesson plan:

　　0 = Insufficient　　　　1 = Developing　　　　2 = Proficient

Element	M	T	W	Th	F	Overall Rating
State **Standards** are identified						----------
Learning Progressions included with supporting standards						----------
Instructional strategies are cognitively aligned						----------
Active Engagement of students is planned						----------
Checks for understanding are planned throughout						----------
Guided and Independent Practice are included						----------
Assessments are cognitively aligned						----------

Area of Strength: 　　　　　　　　　　　　　　　　　　Avg. Score _____

Area of Opportunity for Development:　　　　　　　　　Avg. Score _____

Comments:

Figure 2.3.　Sample Lesson Plan Critique

The critique should, of course, reflect the school's instructional priorities of the instructional team that are mutually agreed upon. In these shared data, the data are not about the singular "you" but about the collective "us." The shared emphasis allows the teachers to grow without feeling threatened by the data and allows teachers to understand that they are not alone in this journey. Again, the shared vision of a system of curriculum and instruction must include this growth mechanism. The same can be said for observation data.

Observations Observations are another vital part of the curriculum and instruction system. Observations provide a snapshot of what is occurring in the classroom. However, that data, when compiled effectively, provide valuable information as to the strengths and weaknesses of the teaching staff. Additionally, when you combine that data with the lesson plan data and correlate the two sets of data, useful information is gleaned on the professional development needs of the staff.

Observation data are utilized best when there is a focus provided for the observations. Westberry (2020) states:

> Teachers should know what the varied foci will be for observations, but not necessarily for each week. For example, one week's focus might be student engagement. The next week's focus might be cognitive level of instructional activities. Another week's focus might be writing activities. The observation forms should reflect the priorities and vision of the leadership. (p. 73)

By providing the focus, the data can be quantified and analyzed, the same as lesson plan data. See Table 2.4, for a sample data analysis for a team's two-week period of observation data.

The aforementioned data show that there are definitively two areas that need some concentration: teacher modeling and cognitive alignment of instructional strategies. An administrator may share these data with the staff so that teachers are aware of the need to focus on these lesson elements. Another two-week period of data may be collected, and if the data are consistent, then professional development may be in order.

The realization of the need to couple lesson plan data and observation data is pivotal to growth. Teachers can plan a lesson beautifully but not deliver it to expectation. The reverse is true. Teachers may execute a lesson to perfection,

Table 2.4. Sample Observation Data Analysis from Observations

Focus	Observation Data February 1 to February 16, 2020				
	Observations	Insufficient	Developing	Proficient	Area of Focus
Instructional Expectations are clear	12	3	1	8	
Teacher **Modeling**	14	6	1	7	Yes
Cognitive Alignment of Instructional Strategies	14	9	2	3	Yes
Effective **Questioning** Techniques utilized	12	2	2	10	

but the planning falls short. The way to ensure that the data are useful is to align the observation tool, of course. Observation tools can change, depending on the focus of the observation. The cumulative effect, however, should be aligned to your state's evaluation instrument. Each focus should be revisited multiple times throughout the year by the instructional team in order to ensure accurate data.

When considering observations, one must consider informal versus formal observations as well. In order to manage observations, an observation schedule should be created to ensure that a true representation of the school is observed and that the same teachers are not observed over and over. It is too easy to run to the gym and observe two or more teachers at the same time so that observation requirements can be met! See Table 2.5 for a sample observation schedule.

Teachers should receive feedback about their observations, certainly, just as they do about lesson plans. Without feedback, teachers will give no credence to evaluation instruments or the need to continuing growing professionally. However, the shared data with the school should not be teacher- or even department-specific. Just with lesson plan data, the information should be about the collective "us" not the singular "you." In doing so, teachers do not feel threatened and know they are not alone. The shared data also gives a focus for planning in PLCs.

PLCs plan a guaranteed and viable curriculum so that all students have access to the same knowledge and skills regardless of their teacher. In this manner, equity is being established in school buildings. Without the common planning, students may receive different instruction on different materials, and all students may not be receiving what they need and deserve. In addition, these teacher teams also use evidence of student learning to inform and improve educational practices. Meaning, PLCs use data to inform their instructional practices, and these data should come from the previously mentioned common assessments.

Many schools say that they utilize PLCs but, in reality, they do not. Putting teachers together in a room without a focus for the meeting or expectations for the meeting is a gamble as to whether or not the desired results will be actualized. This is not just true of teachers, but of people, in general. Therefore, PLCs should be given a focus for the time spent together along with a protocol. A protocol is an outline for how members of the PLC spend their time as well as the focus for the time.

Protocols are readily available on the internet. Some of the protocols that exist include the following:

1. Tuning Protocol—provides a reflection of teachers' plans and student assessments to review cognitive alignment.
2. Consultative Protocol—examines student work to determine if outcome is the intended one.
3. Assessment Building Protocol—provides for cognitive alignment of assessments.
4. Data Protocol—provides for analysis of data and recommendations for teaching and learning.

Several sites offer guidance on PLC protocol, such as The School Reform Initiative and Learning Forward. Whatever protocol that is used, teachers need to be trained on the protocol and understand the expectations for the PLC meetings.

PLCs should have an outcome or form that is completed for the protocol used. This outcome needs to be shared with the instructional team, just as lesson plans are shared. The data gleaned from PLCs are also valuable to the instructional team and should be quantified. Feedback should be provided to those PLCs, just like lesson plan and observation data. In order to do so, the instructional team must agree on the protocol to be used and the forms to be used for the PLCs that will provide the information needed.

Again, there are many readily available PLC reporting forms on the internet. Instructional teams should agree on the forms to be utilized that determine how well the PLC functions and how the data is to be mined. In Figure 2.4, the PLC form provides a clear focus, what supports teachers need, and any questions or concerns they may have.

Just as with the other data, a way to compile data is necessary that is quantifiable from PLC forms. A sample of that work is provided in Table 2.5. The data collected from the PLC reporting forms should be shared with the instructional team and follow-up provided, as needed. Additionally, the whole school can, again, receive data on how well PLCs are functioning and what areas need to be addressed. Additional reporting periods will determine if professional development is needed.

PLC FORM
Assessment Building

Meeting Date: _____   Meeting Time: _____

Members Present:	Members Absent:

Were Team Norms Reviewed: YES   NO

Goal of PLC:

Is the assessment being built prior to teaching the standards?   YES   NO

Which standards are to be addressed in the assessment?

What supporting standards are to be taught in the unit?

How many questions per standard are in the assessment?

List any cognitive alignment issues:

Is the assessment complete?   YES   NO

When is the assessment to be given? _____

If assistance is needed, what assistance can the instructional team provide?

Figure 2.4. *Sample PLC Form*

Table 2.5. Sample PLC Data Form for the Instructional Team

	Assessment Building PLC Data Yes = 1 No = 0				
Element	9/3/2020	9/17/2020	9/31/2020	Total	Follow-up
All members present	1	0	1	2	
Norms reviewed and adhered to	0	0	1	0	AP follow-up with PLC about importance of norms
Goal outlined	1	1	1	1	
Standards identified	1	1	1	1	
Learning progression identified	1	0	0	1	Instructional coach follow-up about learning progressions
Proficiency standards adhered to	0	0	0	1	AP follow up about 80% proficiency
Backward design planning utilized	1	1	1	1	
Assistance needed	0	0	0	0	

Data Meetings The last piece of the curriculum and instruction system is the data meetings. Now, lesson plan data, observation date, and PLC data are shared continuously with the staff. However, standards proficiency needs to be shared with the staff regularly. In doing so, teachers know how to focus remediation for students and also know where the curriculum is missing the mark. Members of the instructional team should be a part of these data meetings, and they should be held regularly. If data meetings are too few, the impact will not be the same.

Think as a parent. You would not currently discipline your child for a behavior they performed six months ago. The learning from the discipline measure would be lost on the child. The same is true for student and teacher learning in school. In order to help teachers remediate the learning lost within a reasonable amount of time, data meetings should be held at least once a month. In doing so, teachers can remediate the standards that were not mastered in a unit soon after the unit's ending, as many units take about a month to complete. If units are shorter, then more meetings are needed.

Table 2.6. Sample Observation Schedule

	9/1–9/8	9/11–9/18	9/21–9/28	10/1–10/8
Principal Smith	Math	English	Math	Science
	Algebra 1	English 1	Geometry	Biology 1
	Algebra 2	English 3	PreCalc	Chemistry
AP Rogers	SS	Foreign Language	SS	Science
	World Geography	Spanish 1	US History	Physics
	Psychology	French 2	Gov/Econ	Earth Science
AP Williams	English	Math	Science	SS
	English 2	Calculus	Biology 2	World History
	English 4	Foundations of Algebra	AP Biology	European History
Instructional Coach	Foreign Language	PE	English	Math
	Spanish 2	PE 1-3	AP Literature	Statistics
	French 1		AP Language	Intermediate Algebra
			Children's Lit	AP Calc
			Creative Writing	

These data meetings should focus on the department as well. What standards did all third-grade English language arts teachers not meet proficiency in the last unit? How can the learning recovery best be addressed? If two third-grade teachers did not meet proficiency but three did, discussions on best practices for teaching those standards should ensue. Teachers should trust the instructional team and each other so that these conversations are fruitful. If all teachers are hitting the mark of proficiency on all unit assessments, something is off.

The focus of the data meetings is to determine exactly what kids know and do not know, the best way to remediate the learning, and what support teachers need to effectively enact learning remediation. Are additional materials needed or does the curriculum unit need to be revised? These meetings are not punitive for teachers as they are part of the growth process. No teacher can be perfect every time they teach. The best teachers can plan a beautiful lesson and execute it to perfection, and the students still may not meet proficiency. Students have different needs, and no one can fulfill all needs every day. Therefore, the focus should be on what you do with the data, not what the data says. This is how trust is built.

SUMMARY

To begin a system of curriculum and instruction, one must first understand curriculum and have fully developed curriculum maps and planning maps. In addition, the instructional team must be identified based on expertise and administrative roles. Once those are established, then an instructional team can focus on the progress monitoring of the system. Elements of the system include the following: curriculum maps, lesson plans, observations, PLCs, and data meetings.

Each element must have a reporting mechanism in order to provide feedback. Data collection tools for each element must also be created. In doing so, teachers know clearly the expectations for all elements and can use the data gleaned to support professional learning and student achievement. The way in which data are shared determines the trust that is built among the faculty and support for the vision of the instructional team.

REFLECTION QUESTIONS

1. What elements of curriculum maps exist in your school and district?
2. Who is a member of the instructional team?
3. What responsibilities do those members have?
4. Are PLCs functioning as intended in your school? If not, how can they be adjusted?
5. What data are used in a system of curriculum and instruction?
6. How are that data shared among the faculty?
7. What elements of a curriculum and instruction system exist in your school? What is missing? What needs to be refined?
8. How can trust be better built surrounding data and professional growth?

REFERENCES

Ainsworth, L. (2011). *Rigorous curriculum design: How to create curricular units of study that align standards, instruction, and assessment.* New York: Houghton Mifflin Harcourt.

Crocco, M. S., & Costigan, A. T. (2007). The narrowing of curriculum and pedagogy in the age of accountability urban educators speak out. *Urban Education, 42*(6), 512–35.

DuFour, R. & Eaker, R. (1998). *Professional communities at cork: Best practices for enhancing student achievement.* Bloomington, IN: Solution Tree Press.

Fuller, E. (2012). *Examining principal turnover*. Retrieved March 1, 2019 from http://nepc.colorado.edu/blog/examining-principal-turnover.

Hopkins, K., Kroning, M., & Kobes, P. (2021). Leadership's role in curriculum revision. *Teaching and Learning in Nursing, 16*(2), 166–68.

Mulenga, I. M., & Mwanza, C. (2019). Teacher's voices crying in the school wilderness: Involvement of secondary school teachers in curriculum development in Zambia. *Journal of Curriculum and Teaching, 8*(1), 32–39.

Olivia, P. F., (2005). *Developing the curriculum*, fifth edition. New York: HarperCollins.

Popham, J. (2003). *Test better, teach better: The instructional role of assessment*. Alexandria, VA: Association for Supervision and Curriculum Development.

Reeves, D. B. (2001). Standards make a difference: The influence of standards on classroom assessment. *NASSP Bulletin, 85*(621), 5–12, https://doi.org/10.1177/019263650108562102.

Tyre, P. (2015, September 26). Why do more than half of principals quit after 5 years? (Rep.). Retrieved March 1, 2019, from Hechinger Report website: https://hechingerreport.org/why-do-more-than-half-of-principals-quit-after-five-years/.

Westberry, L. (2020). *Putting the pieces together: A systems approach to school leadership*. Lanham, MD: Rowman & Littlefield.

Chapter Three

Action Research

A Powerful Tool for School Improvement

Gail Gilmore, Renée N. Jefferson,
and Lee Westberry, The Citadel

This chapter will present action research and how it's used as a powerful tool to help twenty-first-century school principals face the challenges of providing internal and external stakeholders with evidence of student learning outcomes and long-term learning. It begins by defining action research, discussing why it is helpful, how to begin, and how the needs assessment of a school's improvement plan (SIP) is a part of the process. Following are descriptions of five action research models that are most commonly used. An example is provided that illustrates best practices for conducting an action research study.

WHAT IS ACTION RESEARCH?

Action research is any systemic inquiry conducted by teachers, administrators, counselors, or others with a vested interest in the teaching and learning process or environment for the purpose of gathering information about how their particular schools operate, how teachers teach, and how their students learn (Mills, 2011). The use of action research is a powerful tool for administrators to understand what is working in schools. Resources are too scarce to waste on things that do not work, and this includes teacher time. Action research bridges authentic school data that are utilized and are teacher-friendly. These authentic data provide a relevant purpose and focus for both the principal and teachers.

To begin, one must understand that improving the performance of schools should include diagnosing and analyzing the data highlighted in a needs assessment and then creating specific, measurable, achievable, relevant, and timely (SMART) goals for the SIP team to address. An example of a SMART goal for literacy for an elementary SIP, for example, may be the following:

students in grade 3 will demonstrate growth in the areas of reading accuracy and fluency by 15 percent as measured by the DRA2 assessment by May 2022.

This SMART goal is attainable and achievable and will help focus the grade 3 team of teachers to work together for success. Once SMART goals have been created, the team will need to identify clear and effective improvement strategies and evidence-based practices that are frequently monitored for their impact on student achievement. Frequent monitoring of student data and the fidelity of implementation of the selected strategies will help teachers and administrators understand how to adjust and best meet the needs of their students. This is the foundation of data driven decision-making.

Many schools utilize teacher professional learning communities (PLCs) or data teams to monitor learning through classroom assessments. According to Dufour (2004), PLCs involve a systemic process in which teachers work together to analyze and improve the classroom practice. Teachers work in teams, engaging in an ongoing cycle of questions that provider deep team learning. Teachers collaborate and share with colleagues their best practices to better meet the needs of all children. This process leads to higher levels of student achievement.

Much of the work of action research can be performed in these same PLCs. If teachers are focused on student learning and the strategies that yield the best results, then research is being conducted when best practices are highlighted. Of course, the goals, as stated previously, must be based on the deficiencies in learning found in the school. If the deficiency is noted, then research should be conducted on the best strategies to lessen the specific deficiency. PLCs are where the fidelity of implementation and progress monitoring occur.

Why Is It Helpful?

Action research is a powerful tool that principals can use collectively with their teachers to cultivate their craft, improve student performance, and act on what they have learned. Of course, learning should be shared with other colleagues within the school and the district.

Principals can lead by example in their schools and model the use of action research. At principal meetings, administrators can share their findings with other administrators. Action research can become a part of the culture of these meetings and be promoted as a best practice. Nancy Dana (2009), author of *Top 5 Reasons for School Leaders to Engage in Action Research* and *Leading with Passion and Knowledge: The Principal as Action Researcher*, presents an impactful case study to illustrate why principals need to embrace action research.

The case study Dana cites is from a middle school principal in Lake Butler, Florida, who identified a need for an inclusion model in his school. The inclusion model provided both a regular education and special education teacher teaching together in the same classroom or coteaching, to meet the needs of both the mainstream students and the special education students. The principal learned that the regular education students placed in the same classroom as the special education students performed as well or better than their counterparts on various measures of student achievement. This finding became the springboard for change in the principal's school. Teachers embraced the outcomes and accepted the coteaching inclusive model.

Roland Barth (1990), in his book *Improving Schools Within: Teachers, Parents and Principals Can Make the Difference*, writes that action research can bring principals out of isolation: "Principals, like teachers, need and treasure collegiality and peer support. Yet, perhaps even more than teachers, principals live in a world of isolation. This isolation keeps principals from learning, growing, and becoming the best administrators they can be" (p. 192). Too often principals feel alone in their jobs and tend not to reach out to others for fear of appearing inept (Westberry, 2020). Action research models can unite school administrators with a common cause and need to work together.

According to Barth:

> Perhaps the most powerful reason for principals to be learners as well as teachers . . . is the extraordinary influence of modeling behavior. Do as I do, as well as I say, is a winning formula. If principals want students and teachers to take learning seriously, they must be head teachers, or instructional leaders, they must above all else be head learners. (p. 71)

Principals are change agents and must exhibit qualities to move teachers forward. Promoting action research in their schools will propel achievement.

Authors Andy Hargreaves and Michael Fullan (1998) describe how teachers and principals fall into a trap of being "projectiles" (p. 42). They cite that, when seeking school improvement efforts, principals become frantic and pursue quick-fix measures and the silver bullet. Too often, principals are looking for the one size fits all, which is nonexistent. Principals must pause, step back, and look at the big picture. When principals engage in action research, they seek to resolve a problem of practice (PoP) with a clear and planned focus for sustainable outcomes and build a culture of collaboration in their schools.

THE PROCESS

The objective of action research is to provide principals with systematic ways to deal with issues the school faces, such as instructional practices, social issues within schools, student behavior, or academic performance. There are many different action research models from which principals can select. However, the majority share common elements.

Action research models typically contain the following:

- A problem of practice or topic
- The examination of current practices (i.e., existing data)
- A needs assessment that highlights the area of deficiency
- Implementation of researched best practices
- Collection of data on intervention
- Analysis and synthesis of data
- Recommendations (Hendricks, 2017)

Problem of Practice

A PoP is an identified need in teaching and learning that needs improving. It is observable in the classroom and can be found in the student learning data. Once identified, the PoP is presented to the PLC or data team with collected evidence about the students' performance and focus areas of improvement. Teachers discuss the assessments administered, collected, reviewed, and analyzed, and brainstorm ways for improved outcomes. Collectively, the teachers focus on what kind of learning they want to see for their students.

Teachers should review the results of the assessments and engage in dialogue with each other to promote and stimulate deeper thinking. Some possible PoP questions may be as follows:

1. Why are males underperforming females in sixth-grade science? How can we further support these students?
2. How can our English as a second language students be supported more to improve ELA scores?
3. How can we broaden our Tier 1 interventions to reduce the number of students moving to Tier 2 interventions?

Focusing on an instructional issue for a PoP will bring about actionable steps in real time. Since they are actionable and practical, teachers are motivated to work together for change. The purpose of a PoP is to surface a need and make a significant difference in student learning. It contributes to collegial collaboration, reflective practices, and leverages continuous improvement efforts in schools.

A Comprehensive Needs Assessment for School Improvement/Renewal Plans

The SIP is unique to the demographic needs of each and every school. Plans will differ with the needs assessment tools, instruments, and surveys utilized to assess outcomes of student growth and achievement over time, school environment and culture, parent and community engagement and participation, and so on. Student achievement results can be derived from common formative assessments, benchmark assessments, and district- and state-mandated testing. Surveys can be created by the school, district, or state. In all cases, data should be analyzed to recognize patterns of behavior.

The SIP must be aligned with the district goals outlined in the strategic plan, which in turn must meet state guidelines and regulations. If a district's focus is on literacy, then a SIP may identify trends in literacy by grade level or subgroups of students based on ethnicity, poverty levels, gender, and the like to identify any gaps that may exist. If a gap does exist, the SIP team may focus its action research agenda on the deficiencies found.

To align with the areas of deficiency, a timetable is established for administration and data collection. During teacher PLCs and/or grade-level data team meetings, teachers and administrators review the data collectively to determine the students meeting proficiency and those who need additional support. This analysis helps inform the teachers of their instructional focus.

After careful analysis, it is determined what percentage of students meet the assessment goal/proficiency and what percentage of students need additional support. SMART goals and an action plan are created to document steps with strategic instructional strategies, skills, and best practices, to target the needs for improvement. The results of the data analysis provide the SIP team and teachers with critical data for teaching and learning.

From these analysis outcomes, key recommendations will be made to target those specific areas of need for continued improvement efforts. The SIP team may disaggregate the data to determine specific needs of the school's student population, such as special education students, 504 (accommodations and learning aids), socioeconomic status, English learners, and/or talented and gifted. Once the SIP team has interpreted and analyzed the data with the teachers, the principal will present the findings to the faculty, the superintendent, the board of education, parents, and the community at large. SIPs target areas of continuous need and improvement.

Research Best Practices

Every student deserves to receive the very best possible education, and the public demands rigorous results from every educational system. Research best practices in education are based on sound research and professional judgment. Best practices must have a proven track record of success and sustainability and be derived from the principles of professional practice. Research-based practices should be evaluated in different contexts to ensure applicability across schools.

Action research is a proven research-based practice. When school principals and teachers implement interventions from their SIP that have been empirically tested, there is an increased opportunity for greater student success. Scientifically-based research results are based on logic, not opinion, fads, or bias. The methods used are reliable, valid, and informed practice. Overall, when school principals use evidence-based best practices or research, students are more likely to be successful. Research best practices must be utilized at every school level for all students.

Some of the places to review research-based practices include What Works Clearinghouse, which is sponsored by the National Center for Education Evaluation and Regional Assistance (https://ies.ed.gov/ncee/wwc/). This site offers insight into best practices relating to reading, math, dropout prevention, and the like. Other sites that are frequently used are the Promising Practices Network (http://www.promisingpractices.net) and Social Programs That Work (https://evidencebasedprograms.org).

In addition to these sites, researchers may utilize Google Scholar. When searching terms in Google Scholar, one may review primary research pertaining to the identified PoP. Lastly, researchers may also review books such as John Hattie's (2009) *Visible Learning* and other professional publications.

Data Analysis and Recommendations

Once practices are implemented, an evaluation of effectiveness is the next step. Not only should researchers examine the results of the new strategies, but they should also examine their implementation. Fidelity of implementation will have a huge impact on results. Therefore, evaluation should include not only the achievement results but also the process and implementation.

Evaluation results should then inform decisions that are made. Decisions that are based on data are best because they are more likely to improve outcomes for students and teachers. Teachers want to feel impactful and valued for their crafts, therefore, data-driven decision-making sets both teachers and students up for success.

ACTION RESEARCH MODELS

There are many models you can use to conduct action research that range in levels of complexity. The following five models are included because they are used most frequently in educational research focusing on PreK–12 schools.

The first two models are Stringer's (2007) *Action Research Interacting Spiral* and Bachman's (2001) *Action Research Spiral* (as cited in Stringer, 2007), which involve a three-step action research process. The third model is Riel's (2007) four-step *Action Research Model*. The last two models involve a seven-step process and are Lewin's (1946) *Action Research Spiral* and McKernan's (1996) *Action Research Model*. The specific steps of each model are presented in Table 3.1.

Which action research model should a principal use? If one looks at the steps of the five models in Table 3.1, they are essentially variations on the same theme as evidenced by their shared elements (Hendricks, 2017, p. 15). For example, each of the five models begins with an idea or topic and includes the following:

- Gathering relevant information (i.e., data) to describe the current status
- Analyzing the information collected
- Interpreting the results and explaining how or why things are the way they are, that is, theorizing or hypothesizing
- Developing and implementing a plan of action
- Evaluating data from the action plan
- Reflecting on the action plan process and results
- Preparing for the next action plan.

Table 3.1. Steps of Five Action Research Models

Stringer (2007)	Bachman (2001)	Riel (2007)	Lewin (1946)	McKernan (1996)
Step 1: Look	Plan	Study and Plan	Identify a problem	Define general or initial idea
Step 2: Think	Act and Observe	Act	Reconnaissance or fact finding	Needs assessment
Step 3: Act	Reflect	Collect and Analyze Evidence	Planning	Hypothesize, Generate Ideas
		Reflect	Take first action step	Develop action plan
			Evaluate	Implement plan
			Amend plan	Evaluate action
			Take a second step	Make decisions (reflect, explain, understand action)

These models are designed to be iterative, cyclical, or spiral processes that can help principals reflect on practices, take action, reflect on the actions taken, take further action, and continue the "action, reflection" process to ensure positive personal, professional, and organizational change (Riel, 2019). The action research model a principal should use depends on the nature of the problem to solve or condition to improve and the urgency to identify solutions or make improvements.

Simple Action Research Models

An example illustrating Stringer's (2017) three-step action research process will be used to compare and contrast the steps of the four other models (Bachman, 2001; Lewin, 1946; McKernan, 1996; Riel, 2019). Suppose a high school principal's SIP includes the objective to implement best practices that may be used in reading and writing instruction for tenth-grade students. The principal notes that one of the areas in need of improvement is personalized instructional strategies and interventions on a regular basis so that each student can reach his or her true potential.

Using Stringer's (2007) *Action Research Interacting Spiral*, the principal begins by deciding what information is needed to assess the current status of the tenth-grade students' reading and writing levels (Step 1, **Look**). The information is then gathered. For example, results from Response to Intervention (RTI) for literacy assessment scores, writing samples, observations, and teacher interviews. In the second step, **Think**, the principal analyzes and interprets the information gathered and identifies possible reasons and explanations.

Keep in mind that the information will present things that are going well, things that may need a little improvement, and things that need a lot of improvement. It is at this step that the principal prioritizes the list of actions. The principal may share the list with the administrative team or leadership team and ask them to submit a prioritized list of actions to be considered, or the principal and the administrative or leadership team may prioritize the list of actions together.

The third and the final step of Stringer's (2007) model, **Act**, is for the principal, working in conjunction with the administrative team, to develop, implement, and evaluate an action plan. Once the focus of the action plan is determined, then it is time to decide what data are needed to make informed decisions. Suppose the action plan involves modifying an RTI instructional strategy to examine its effectiveness in improving reading comprehension for the tenth graders who read below grade level. All tenth-grade English teachers will use the same modified RTI strategy for literacy with their students who read below grade level.

Examples of data to collect include students' performance on assessments, interviews with teachers about the modified strategy, observations conducted by the reading specialist, and interviews with students about their perspectives. After the data are collected and analyzed, the principal evaluates the action plan. Based on the evaluation, the principal may decide to continue using the modified instructional strategy or make additional modifications for a revised action plan.

Applying Bachman's (2001) *Action Research Spiral*, the principal's first step is **Plan,** that is (1) decide what information is needed to assess the current status of the tenth-grade students' reading and writing levels; (2) gather the relevant data (e.g., assessment scores and writing samples); and (3) describe what the data represent. This step also includes analyzing the data gathered and making interpretations to explain the current status of the tenth-grade students' reading and writing levels.

The principal implements the action plan during Bachman's second step, **Act and Observe**. For example, the tenth-grade English teachers begin using the modified instructional strategy; students then complete related assessments; and the reading specialist observes implementation of the modified strategy. Data analysis and interpretation also occur during this step. Evaluation of the action research study occurs during Bachman's third step, **Reflect**.

So, what is the difference between Bachman (2001) and Stringer's (2007) action research models? The difference is the implementation of the action research plan. In Bachman's model, the implementation occurs during Step 2 (**Act and Observe**) and during Step 3 (**Act**) in Stringer's model. For principals, whether data collection occurs during Step 2 or Step 3 is not as important as the purpose of the action plan and the time line for implementation and decision-making. Since both models provide a three-step process for conducting action research, it appeals to principals who want a simple model and are able to identify the specific actions within each step.

For principals needing more detail regarding specific actions, a more complex model should be considered. In this context, complexity means a model with more steps. Riel (2007) views action research as "a collaborative process as it is done WITH people in a social context and understanding the change means probing multiple understandings of complex social systems" (p. 1). Using the example where the high school principal's objective is to implement best practices that may be used in reading and writing instruction for tenth-grade students, the principal begins by creating an action research team.

For example, the team may include two or three tenth-grade English teachers, reading specialist, school counselor, and an assistant principal of instruction. With a collaborative action research model, the principal is part of the action research team. Step 1 of Riel's model is **Study and Plan** where relevant data are collected, analyzed, interpreted, and used to explain the current status of tenth-grade students' reading and writing levels.

Step 2 is **Take Action**, and this is when the action plan is developed by the action research team. As previously described, the plan involves modifying an RTI instructional strategy to examine its effectiveness in improving reading comprehension for tenth graders who read below grade level. Decisions such as the types of data to be collected, development of the data collection instruments, and the time line for implementation are made. The action plan is implemented in Step 3, **Collect and Analyze Evidence**.

After the data are collected and analyzed, the action research team makes decisions regarding the effectiveness of the modified RTI instructional strategy. In Step 4, **Reflect**, the team reflects on each step of the model, for example, the collaborative process of gathering information and determining the focus of the action plan, developing the data collection instruments, and the procedures used to administer the instruments and collect data.

The components of an action research study presented in Riel's (2007) four-step action research model are the same components included in Bachman (2001) and Stringer's (2007) three-step models. The difference is Riel's step for developing the action research plan (Step 2, **Take Action**) is a separate step from collecting and analyzing the data (Step 3, **Collect and Analyze Evidence**). For principals, the purpose of the action plan and the time line for implementation and decision-making are factors that affect the time frame for developing and implementing an action research study.

So, which of the three action research models should a principal use? If you want a simple model, you may select a three-step model (Bachman, 2001; Stringer, 2007) or Riel's four-step model. If you are looking for a model with more detail, Lewin's (1946) *Action Research Spiral* or McKernan's (1996) *Action Research Model* should be considered.

Complex Action Research Models

The two complex models to be discussed are Lewin's (1946) *Action Research Spiral* and McKernan's (1996) *Action Research Model*. The steps of each model will be described using the example where the high school principal selects an objective (*To implement best practices that may be used in reading and writing instruction for tenth-grade students*) and an area in need of improvement (*personalized instructional strategies and interventions*) from the SIP.

For Lewin's seven-step model, the principal begins by **Identifying a General or Initial Idea** (Step 1), which is improving personalized instructional strategies and interventions for tenth-grade students who read below grade level. Next, the principal gathers relevant information such as RTI for literacy assessment scores and observational data from the reading specialist to assess current performance (Step 2, **Reconnaissance or Fact Finding**).

In Step 3 (**Planning**), the principal develops the action research plan, that is, to modify an RTI instructional strategy. This step includes things like professional development for the tenth-grade English teachers on the modified instructional strategy and developing instruments to collect data.

Step 4 (**Take First Action Step**) is when data collection occurs. The principal may decide to collect data for two weeks and then conduct an evaluation of the action plan (Step 5, **Evaluate**) to see how teachers are doing and how students are responding to the modified instructional strategy. Based on the feedback from teachers, students, and reading specialists, changes may be needed, for example, students may respond better to peer learning (Step 6, **Amended Plan**).

Step 7 (**Take a Second Action Step**) involves collecting data for the amended action research plan. The principal evaluates the amended plan to see if further changes are required. Based on the evaluation outcome, the action research plan can be completed or become an ongoing process.

McKernan's (1996) action research model also has seven steps. In Step 1, the principal **defines the problem**, which is to improve personalized instructional strategies and interventions for tenth-grade students who read below grade level. In Step 2, the **Needs Assessment**, the principal gathers information to assess the current abilities of tenth-grade students who read below grade level; to learn what instructional methods, strategies, or interventions have already been used; and to identify what gaps in leaning remain (McCawley, 2009).

The results of the needs assessment are used to generate ideas and develop hypotheses on how to help students improve in reading (Step 3, **Hypotheses and Ideas**). This process helps the principal **develop the action plan** (Step 4), which is to modify an RTI instructional strategy currently used with tenth-grade students who read below grade level.

The action research **plan is implemented** in Step 5. Examples of data that can be collected by the principal include (1) feedback from tenth-grade English teachers about using the modified instructional strategies, (2) RTI for literacy assessment scores, and (3) grades from teacher-developed assessments.

Step 6 (**Evaluate action**) occurs after the action plan has been implemented. During this step, the principal shares the results and requests feedback from tenth-grade English teachers, students, reading specialists, and assistant principal of instructional practices. Lastly, Step 7 (**Decisions**) involves reflecting on the steps taken, explaining outcomes, and understanding what occurred during each step of the action plan process.

Which Action Research Model Should Principals Use?

When selecting an action research model, whether it is one presented in this chapter or in other literature, principals should consider the purpose of the action plan, the time required to implement the plan, and the type of decision to be made. The best place to start is with the SIP since it includes short- and long-term goals and objectives, areas of strength, areas in need of improvement, and strategies.

It may seem that short-term goals and objectives would be better addressed with simple action research models such as Bachman's (2007) and Riel's (2007). Long-term goals and objectives may be better addressed by utilizing complex models such as Lewin's (1946) and McKernan's (1996). However, this assumption is misleading since the models include the same components for conducting an action research study. Principals should select a model based on how they process information.

For principals who prefer information to be organized by a few broad categories, a simple action research model is recommended; and a complex model is recommended for principals who prefer information to be presented in detail-specific categories. Additionally, a major difference is the time frame for the project. Of course, school improvement is an effort better realized when teams share the work and develop solutions. However, the multistep processes that include teams take more time.

The important thing for principals to remember is that, regardless of the action research model selected, developing and implementing an action plan leads to school improvement, and that is the ultimate goal.

A SAMPLE ACTION RESEARCH STUDY

This example on how to conduct an action research study is based on the best practices from the models presented in the chapter and those used by educational action researchers. A fictitious scenario based on data presented in the needs assessment of a SIP for an elementary school is used to demonstrate the seven-step process of the action research study:

1. Define the problem or area of SIP
2. Conduct a needs assessment
3. Develop hypotheses or ideas
4. Develop an action plan
5. Implement the plan

6. Evaluate the plan
7. Make decisions (reflect, explain)

The scenario is presented first, then demographic characteristics of the school are presented in Table 3.2. Table 3.3 shows students' at or above and below the benchmark on DRA2+. The readiness levels on a state reading test for Grades 3, 4, and 5 are presented in Figure 3.1, and Figure 3.2 shows Grade 3 students' performance on a state's reading standards. In Table 3.4, the elementary school example is used to illustrate what principals should *do* and *consider* for each of the nine action research steps.

Scenario

A snapshot of 2016 and 2017 data from an elementary SIP is used to illustrate how principals can implement action research. The snapshot includes demographic characteristics and the percentage change in characteristics between 2016 and 2017 (see Table 3.2) and performance of students in Grades 3, 4, and 5 on a formative and a summative achievement assessment. The formative assessment is Development Reading Assessment, Second Edition PLUS (DRA2+), a national formative reading assessment through which teachers systematically observe, record, and evaluate changes in student reading performance (see Table 3.2). A standardized state reading test provides summative data in English language arts for all students in Grades 3, 4, and 5 (see Figure 3.1) and on literary text and informational text performance for the third graders (see Figure 3.2).

Table 3.2. Demographic Characteristics of Elementary School

Demographic Characteristics	2016	2017	Two-Year Change
45-Day Average Daily Membership	N = 295	N = 280	−15.0
Teacher Attendance (%)	98.9	97.0	−1.9
Student Attendance (%)	97.9	96.7	−1.2
Ethnicity: Black (%)	82.3	80.7	−1.6
Ethnicity: White (%)	1.9	4.5	2.6
Ethnicity: Other (%)	15.8	14.9	−0.9
Poverty Index (%)	93.5	90.3	−3.2
Special Education (%)	17.6	14.15	3.5
Limited English Proficient (%)	16.7	15.5	−1.2
Retention Rate (%)	0.6	0.3	−0.3
Suspension Rate (%)	13.2	14.2	1.0

Table 3.3. Percentage At or Above and Below Benchmark on DRA2+

Performance Level	2016	2017	Two-Year Change
At or Above Benchmark (%)	77.6	94.6	17
Below Benchmark (%)	22.4	5.4	17
Total (%)	100	100	

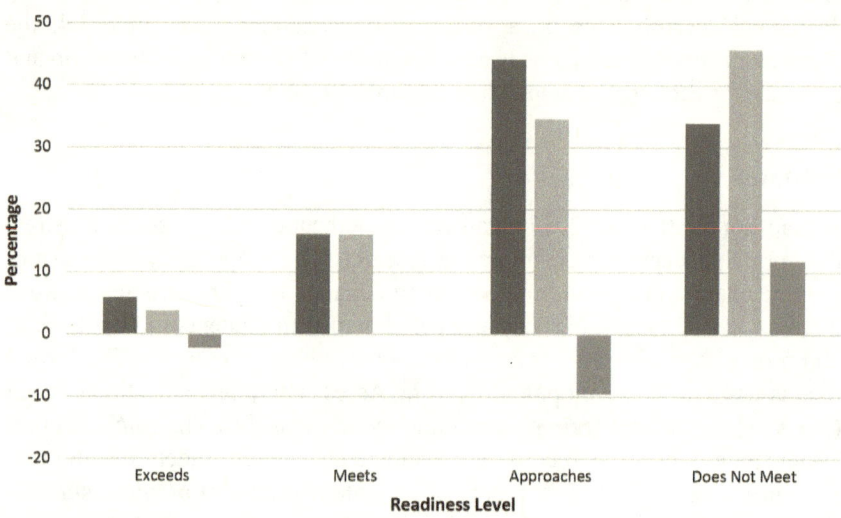

Figure 3.1. Readiness Levels on State Reading Test for Grades 3, 4, and 5

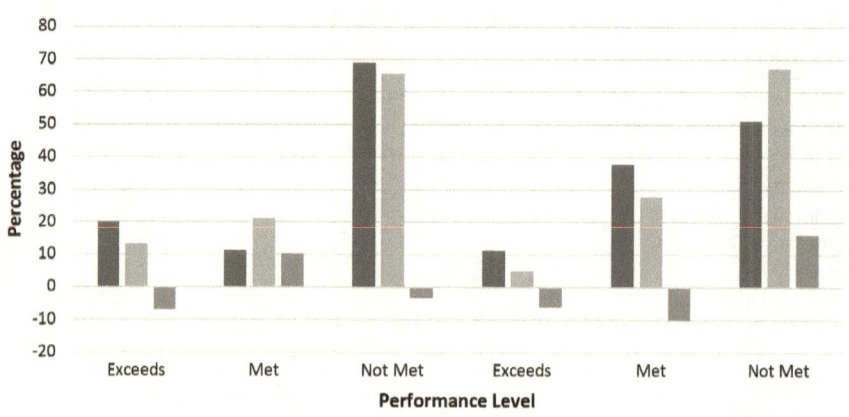

Figure 3.2. Performance on State Reading Standards for Grade 3 Students

Table 3.4. Action Research Steps Based on Elementary School Example

Steps	What to Do and Consider	Elementary School Example
Step 1	Do: Define the problem, situation, or areas identified in your SIP. Consider: What do you want to investigate, examine, or explore? Will you use a research question, objective, or hypothesis?	SIP Area: Reading Informational Text Purpose: To investigate instructional materials and strategies used in informational text learning for all Grade 3 students. Research Question: How do instructional materials and strategies used with informational text impact the academic performance of Grade 3 students? Rationale: The percentage of all students in Grades 3, 4, and 5 in the Does Not Meet category increased 11.8% between 2016 (33.9%) and 2017 (45.7%) on the state reading test. The percentage of Grade 3 students decreased 3.3% in the Not Met category for literary text between 2016 (68.9%) and 2017 (65.6%) on the state reading test. The percentage of Grade 3 students increased 16.1% in the Not Met category between 2016 (51.1%) and 2017 (67.2%) on the state reading test.
Step 2	Do: Conduct needs assessment. Consider: What areas of need are identified in your needs assessment? Do you have existing data (e.g., school data you collect or receive)? Who has access to current school data (e.g., benchmark, standardized, or common assessments)?	Areas of Need: Examine academic performance for reading strategies used to teach informational text to Grade 3 students (e.g., asking and answering questions based on key details in the text, summarizing main points of the story, and analyzing cause and effect relationships). Identify learning gaps for reading strategies. Existing Data/Documents: (1) Grade 3 item analysis for state reading test; and (2) item analysis of teacher-created assessments for informational text.
Step 3	Do: Develop hypotheses or ideas.	Ideas from needs assessment: Learning gaps occur when (1) asking and answering questions based on key details in the text, (2) summarizing main points of the story, and (3) analyzing cause and effect relationships are used. Add variety to reading instruction. Use strategies that are easy to implement and that help keep students actively engaged (e.g., Repeat and Speak, Allow Think Time, and Employ the 3-2-1 Strategy).

(continued)

Table 3.4. *(continued)*

Steps	What to Do and Consider	Elementary School Example
Step 4	Do: Develop action plan.	Action Research Team: (1) Two or three Grade 3 teachers, (2) reading specialist, (3) teacher-librarian, (4) principal and/or assistant principal
	Consider Participants: Who will provide the data needed for your action research study (e.g., students, parents, teachers, school counselors, teacher-librarians, administrators, or parents)?	Participants: (1) students, (2) teachers, parents, (3) reading specialist, and (4) teacher-librarian
	Consider Data Needed: What types of quantitative data do you plan to collect? What types of qualitative data do you plan to collect? Will you collect data using a survey, observation checklist, interview, or documents?	Data Needed: (1) teacher instructional strategies used with informational text for individual students and groups; (2) student grades based on written assessment; (3) student grades based on oral assessment; (4) student grades after peer learning based on written and oral assessments; (5) teacher-librarian instructional strategies used with informational text; (6) types of parental reinforcement of informational text; and (7) teacher and reading specialist recommendations
	Consider Data Collection Plan: Who will create the instrument(s)? How will you pilot-test the instrument to make sure you collect the data that is needed? Who will analyze the data?	Data Collection Plan: (1) develop focus group interview questions for teachers; (2) develop individual and focus group interview questions for students; (3) develop telephone interview questions for parents; (4) pilot-test all instruments; (5) decide how and who will collect data; and (6) determine data analysis techniques
	Consider: Will you use formative or summative data, or both for a holistic approach?	Formative and summative assessments will be used.

Steps	What to Do and Consider	Elementary School Example
Step 5	Do: Implement plan. Consider: How will you monitor the data collection process? Who will collect and compile the data?	Data to Collect: (1) focus group interviews with Grade 3 teachers, reading specialist, and teacher-librarian; (2) individual and focus group interviews with students; and (3) telephone interview with parents
	Consider Data Analysis: Will data be disaggregated to determine specific needs of the school's student population? If you have qualitative data, will you need to code textual data, visual, or audio data? Do you need to purchase content analysis software? If you have quantitative data, will you need descriptive, parametric, nonparametric statistics? Are you able to use Excel or do you need a statistical package for social sciences SPSS?	Data Analysis: (1) state reading test item analysis—frequencies and percentages; (2) informational text oral and written assessments item analysis—frequencies and percentages; (3) informational text oral and written assessments —frequencies, percentages, means, and standard deviations; (4) interviews—content analysis; (5) t-Test to test differences between two means; (6) ANOVA to test mean differences for three or more classes; and (7) chi-square test to test differences among categories
	Consider Data Visualization: Do some or all of the results require narrative descriptions? Can some of the results be displayed graphically using pie charts, histograms, or tables?	Data Visualization: Examine results of disaggregated data to determine if they address research question: (1) narrative descriptions of textual data; (2) bar graphs to compare things between different groups like frequencies and track changes over time; (3) pie charts for data with two to five categories that compose the whole; (4) line graphs to track changes over time; and (5) tables for some textual data.
	Consider Results: Do the results provide information needed to address the school improvement area of need, research question, objective, or hypothesis?	Interpretation of Results: (1) Show most relevant results in graphs, figures, or tables, (2) summarize key results from narrative data, (3) use triangulation to test the consistency of findings obtained from different data collection instruments.

(continued)

Table 3.4. *(continued)*

Steps	What to Do and Consider	Elementary School Example
Step 6	Do: Evaluate plan. Consider: What are the various perspectives (e.g., teachers, administrators, other school personnel) on developing and implementing the action research plan? Did the questions of data collection instruments provide responses needed to make decisions? Were there unexpected disruptions during data collection?	Evaluation: Conduct informal evaluations throughout the action research plan (e.g., checking progress throughout data collection). Conduct formal evaluations at specific intervals throughout the data collection (e.g., every two to three weeks to assess progress).
Step 7	Do: Make decisions (reflect, explain, understand action) Consider: Did the action research plan provide information needed to address the school improvement area of need, research question, objective, or hypothesis?	Decisions: Did instructional materials and strategies used with informational text improve academic performance of Grade 3 students? If yes, will you continue to use the materials and strategies? If no, what materials and strategies will you try next? Are there other factors that may have affected Grade 3 students' performance?
	Consider Reporting Findings: What format will be used to present the findings of your action research (e.g., written report, oral presentation, or both)? How will findings be presented to teachers, colleagues, administrators, parents, superintendent of schools, and board of education	Reporting Findings: (1) Oral and written reports to teachers at faculty meeting; (2) oral report to colleagues; (3) written report to Superintendent of Schools; and (4) SIP

Source: Adapted from McKernan's (1996) *Action Research Model*.

SUMMARY

Action research is a cutting-edge practice and when used by principals collaboratively, it will encourage, inspire, and motivate teachers, school counselors, and other school personnel to reflect on and refine educational policies and practices for school improvement. This chapter demonstrated how principals can use SIP and needs assessment to conduct action research based on best practices.

The steps involved in conducting action were defined and illustrated using a scenario based on a snapshot of data from a SIP. Principals are responsible for continuously engaging their teachers (school counselors, teacher-librarians, and other school personal) in instructional dialogue and reflective practices, so that they are best equipped to improve teaching and learning.

Action research is a powerful tool that can help principals critically examine and understand current practices within a timely manner; promote relationship building while fostering a sense of community; and is a practical, relevant, and authentic way to engage in school improvement.

REFLECTION QUESTIONS

1. What elements of your SIP will you implement in action research?
2. How will you introduce action research to your faculty? Parents? Community?
3. Will the members of your school improvement team need professional development in action research? If so, what specific focus with the action research process will they need?
4. How will action research become a part of your school culture? How will you promote, model, and sustain action research?
5. How will you build leadership capacity around the action research process? Which teacher leaders will lead the charge of action research within the faculty? How will teacher leaders share their learning of action research?
6. What are your needs to continue with action research?
7. How has the use of action research in your school broadened your prospective as a leader? How has the use of action research altered the way you view and approach educational questions and problems?
8. Has action research impacted you by way of viewing and approaching educational practices differently?
9. Has the use of action research promoted stronger relationships and collaboration with your faculty? Provide examples.

REFERENCES

Bachman, L. (2001). *Review of the agricultural knowledge system in Fiji: Opportunities and limitations of participatory methods and platforms to promote innovation development.* Unpublished dissertation. Humboldt University of Berlin, Germany.

Barth, R. (1990). *Improving schools from within: Teachers, parents and administrators can make the difference.* Hoboken, NJ: Jossey-Bass.

Dana, N. F. (n.d.). *Top 5 reasons for school leaders to engage in action research.* Alexandria, VA: AASA.

Dana, N. F. (Ed.). (2009). *Leading with passion and knowledge: The principal as action researcher.* Thousand Oaks, CA: Corwin.

Dufour, R. (2004). Professional learning communities. *Educational Leadership, 61*(8), 6–11.

Hargreaves, A., & Fullan, M. (1998). *What's worth fighting for out there?* New York: Teachers College Press.

Hattie, J. (2009). *Visible learning: A synthesis of over 800 meta-analyses relating to achievement.* New York: Routledge.

Hendricks, C. C. (2017). *Improving schools through action research: A reflective practice approach.* Hoboken, NJ: Pearson.

Lewin, K. (1946). Action research and minority problems. *Journal of Social Issues, 2*(4), 34–36.

McCawley, P. F. (2009). *Methods for conducting educational needs assessment: Guidelines for cooperative extension system professions.* University of Idaho Extension. Retrieved from https://www.extension.uidaho.edu/publishing/pdf/bul/bul0870.pdf

McKernan, J. (1996). *Curriculum action research: A handbook of methods and resources for the reflective practitioner.* Second Edition. London: Kogan Page.

Mills, G. E. (2011). *Action research: A guide for the teacher researcher.* Fourth Edition. Hoboken, NJ: Pearson.

Ontario Education Improvement Commission. (2000). *School improvement planning: A handbook for principals, teachers, and school councils.* Toronto: Ontario Legislative Library.

Riel, M. (2007). Understanding Action Research. The Center for Collaborative Action Research, Pepperdine University. Retrieved from http://cadres.pepperdine.edu/ccar/define.html.

Riel, M. (2019). *Understanding collaborative action research.* Center for Collaborative Action Research, Pepperdine University.

Stringer, E. T. (2007). *Action research interacting spiral.* Thousand Oaks, CA: Sage

Westberry, L. (2020). *Putting the pieces together: A systems approach to school leadership.* Lanham, MD: Rowman & Littlefield.

Chapter Four

Technology Integration
Administrators Leading the Charge
Rachel Biritz, Clemson University

> It is important to remember that educational software, like textbooks, is only one tool in the learning process. Neither can be a substitute for well-trained teachers, leadership, and parental involvement.
>
> —Keith Krueger

Think about the shift to virtual learning when schools shut down during the onset of the COVID-19 pandemic in the spring of 2020. Whether you were a school administrator, a teacher, on the path to becoming a teacher, a student, a school-aged child's parent, or a citizen watching the news at the time, you saw the challenges of shifting to a virtual education system. Some schools had a seamless transition due to technology being thoroughly and effectively integrated into their schools already. Other schools struggled to provide access to information and guide teachers, students, and families into the virtual learning space.

Though the school closures due the COVID-19 pandemic were an exceptional event, it was a reminder to administrators everywhere to think more deeply about the role of technology in their schools on an everyday basis. By understanding how to better lead schools to utilize technology, administrators and instructional leaders can positively impact student learning outcomes daily while also being prepared for any unforeseen events.

Educational and instructional leaders can ensure that students have technological systems in place that will aid, not distract, their learning. For technology to be meaningful in student learning, systems must be fully integrated into the daily habits of a school and its classroom. Through the expansion of administrators' own knowledge, understanding of technology in place, and learning about the possibilities available to their school communities, administrators can make a large impact on student learning.

School administrators play a key role in the long-term role of technology integration, from implementation through continued use. While keeping the realities of challenges that administrators face in their roles, recommendations on how to make improvements at multiple levels will be discussed. Finally, this chapter will suggest possible models for ongoing professional development (PD) for whole schools, groups within schools, neighboring schools, and districts.

THE REALITY OF TECHNOLOGY INTEGRATION IN SCHOOLS

The definition of technology integration from the National Forum on Education Statistics (2002) includes the key terminology of "daily" and "routine" (p. 75). As many educators know and have experienced, technology often gets brought into schools and classrooms, is highly utilized briefly, then fades out months later. This cycle repeats with the next new program/software/tool available. For technology integration to truly happen, multiple levels of ongoing PD must occur. All PDs should begin with and be sustained by school administration.

Typical Barriers to Successful Technology Integration

Comfort Level

Everyone has different comfort levels with technology. Some easily jump right into the latest software without reading the user guide, while others need numerous learning sessions before they feel that they have understood enough to try on their own. This range of comfort obviously creates difficulties when bringing new technology into a school. If the school leader has low comfort with technology, it can present additional challenges from the outset, but it does not have to. For a school leader to successfully lead technology integration, one only needs to be open and willing to learn how to utilize technology effectively.

Other Forms of Resistance

Educators everywhere have experienced fads that roll in then right back out of schools and districts, whether it be a new program or emphasis on a particular skillset (e.g., mathematics word problems, social-emotional learning).

With this pattern engrained in the minds of many teachers, thoroughly learning, and thus integrating, new technology at a school can be met with varying levels of resistance. Additionally, numerous educators are plagued by anxiety over technology and its integration (Howard, 2013).

Kopcha (2012) identified five common barriers that teachers face when integrating technology into their instruction: access (consistency in availability and performance), vision (administrator's vision), beliefs (usefulness, difficulty), time (student management, planning for us, learning the technology), and PD (connection between training and actual classroom practice). Some of these forms of resistance are unconscious reactions. When beginning the technology integration process, it is crucial to attempt to mitigate these forms of resistance to ensure a better chance at successful technology integration.

Pitfalls of Taking a Backseat in Technology Integration

School administrators are bombarded with items to accomplish, so it is reasonable to have someone else lead the charge when integrating new technology. Yet doing so can have consequences. When technology integration is not a top priority on administration's agenda, it is modeled for teachers that it does not need to be a top priority on their agenda either. Teachers' buy-in is one of the clearest ways new technologies are either successfully integrated or used intermittently. Therefore, showing all staff how important technology integration is to administration emphasizes that the technology is important and intended to stick around.

Additionally, when having other personnel lead technology integration, administrators can stray from what is happening on a day-to-day basis with that technology while they focus on other tasks or projects. Losing sight of the happenings of integration can lead to a disconnect between the purpose and vision of bringing in the new technology and its integration. For integration to happen, administrators must be aware of the difficulties being encountered during the roll out of new technology, how students are applying the new technology to their learning, what improvements need to be made across the campus, and what common questions are arising.

When an administrator has someone else leading the technology integration charge, issues that appear are learned of secondhand. It is better to be at the helm of technology integration to mitigate problems as they arise by getting in touch with technology representatives, sending schoolwide emails that answer questions or clarify misconceptions, or scheduling additional PD.

MAKING IMPROVEMENTS AT MULTIPLE LEVELS

There is an abundance of educational software available on the market today. Some programs have been around for some time and have a positive reputation (e.g., Google Classroom, Khan Academy, Code.org, Kahoot!), making it easier to justify their integration into schools. Others are mentioned on social media sites or heard about through word of mouth, making the case for their purchase and integration more challenging. A reliable source of locating meaningful technology based on evidence is the What Works Clearinghouse from the Institute of Education Sciences.

When bringing in something well known or novel for school use, it must be made clear that whatever new technology is being brought in is being done so with the intention of true integration which, again, means that it is to be used on a daily/regular basis. In the end, the technology must clearly align with the vision and goals of your school and keep the students at the forefront of the conversation.

How to Improve Student Outcomes with Technology

At the heart of any educator's role is student learning. As such, the main goal of technology integration in schools is to improve educational outcomes for students. School administrators play a pivotal role as instructional leaders for student outcomes, including as the leader of technology integration. We know that technology is here to stay in education. However, technology in the classroom can be distracting or problematic, which obviously does not aid student learning.

When utilizing technology in a way that enhances student learning, it should improve student outcomes. In thinking about what technology should be integrated into your school, take the time to consider how that technology can be used to engage students and enhance the learning taking place in classrooms. Will it add to what is being taught in classrooms? Or will it be a filler or distraction that does not have a place during instructional time? In a later section, understanding how to evaluate the use of technology will be discussed.

How to Improve Professionally with Technology Integration

Though administrators often participate heavily with the implementation of new technology into their school, it is often the teachers who receive subsequent PD. During PD on new or integrated technology, school administration should be leading or actively participating. This strong role in PD sends multiple messages to school personnel: the administrator is engaged in this work alongside everyone and this work is important enough to be a priority over other tasks.

If you are someone who needs more time with technology to feel confident in using it, show that to your teachers; they will appreciate your authenticity. If you are tech-savvy and can be the person who guides those who have technology anxiety, they will appreciate your mentorship. The key here is being authentic and walking alongside the rest of the staff as technology integration occurs, whether it is day 1 or day 1,000 of integration.

Though not every administrator is best suited to be the go-to person to troubleshoot when something goes awry with technology, the administrator should be the go-to person in finding the correct source to fix problems that arise. Whether it be getting in touch with a representative or sending in a trouble ticket to the district office, school administrator should instantly know who can resolve a problem with technology most efficiently.

Additionally, school administrators should continue to be updated on innovations, price changes, shutdowns for updates, and the like from companies where the technology is purchased from so information can be quickly distributed to personnel that may be impacted. As an additional incentive to be the primary contact for technology integration at their school, administrators who are involved in communications with the companies that sell and maintain educational software are sometimes asked to pilot new programs for free, provide feedback to improve software, and made aware if grant funding becomes available.

Educational software companies are looking to create long-lasting relationships with their clientele, so they look to their clients who have been connecting with them regularly when interesting opportunities arise. Creating these relationships also allows administrators to be alerted to the latest trends and improved options for their students. If your name pops into their mind first because you have built a positive relationship, you will be the first to hear about opportunities that can benefit your students.

As with curriculum, it is expected that principals are aware of updates, changes, and improvements available to better inform instruction. Southworth (2010) notes that teacher leaders need to be able to show they are continuing students of their own work to be effective instructional leaders. Instructional leadership also requires high levels of knowledge and understanding of curricula, pedagogy, and both student and adult learning (Southworth, 2010). Hallinger (2010) notes that managing school instructional programs requires administrators to be "deeply engaged in stimulating, supervising, and monitoring teaching and learning in the school" (p. 66).

With technology being so prevalent in schools today, it is impossible to be a true instructional leader without being heavily invested in the technology that is integrated into your school. You may have to think outside of the box to show how invested you are to staff and students. Read the vignette below about Mrs. Rhodes, an elementary school principal, who got creative in leading her school to integrate new technological software.

Willing to Learn: One Administrator's Journey in Bringing New Software to Classrooms

After determining that one of the major factors in low student mathematics scores at Mrs. Rhodes's elementary school was the lack of fluency in addition, subtraction, multiplication, and division facts, the school purchased a software program that focused on improving student fluency. The program met the needs of each student's current abilities, with automatic adjustments made as students proved mastery of their mathematics facts.

During the implementation of the new software program, teachers and students regularly ran into problems, as they had not yet become thoroughly familiarized with the program. The students would ask their teachers for help, and in turn, teachers would ask for help from their principal, Mrs. Rhodes. Mrs. Rhodes worked closely with the software company to be sure there were not errors within the software, but also wanted to be able to help the teachers and students with their questions.

To learn the program, Mrs. Rhodes first spent time watching her son, who attended her school, while he played the program's games after school. After a few weeks, her son became irritated that she continued to watch over his shoulder. So, Mrs. Rhodes created a student account for herself and spent time viewing the program through the eyes of a student while also competing with her son as they sat side by side during his daily use of the program after school.

Though Mrs. Rhodes did not need to learn mathematics facts, it was important for her that she understood the software program. Mrs. Rhodes was somewhat confident with technology, but the daily use of the program dramatically increased her confidence in navigating the new software from both the student's end and the teacher's end. Mrs. Rhodes's original intention to learn the program was a success; she was able to help the teachers and students in navigating the program smoothly and learned the little-known tricks of using the program more efficiently.

What Mrs. Rhodes did not anticipate was how excited the students would be to know that their principal was using the program too. Her son started telling his classmates about their daily competitions. Then, when logging into the software, the students began to see Mrs. Rhodes's name pop up on the program's leaderboard. Students became determined to beat their principal's score, and her daily score became a part of the morning news show.

Engagement across the school increased and students became more motivated than before to spend time on the program, just like their principal. Mathematics fluency increased across the school, and it was evident in benchmark and end-of-year assessments. Mrs. Rhodes approached technology integration by placing it as a top priority for herself, and in turn, making it top priority schoolwide. By being willing to learn the new program, Mrs. Rhodes impacted student learning in a way she did not anticipate.

How to Improve Teachers' Capacity with Technology

While students are at the center of technology integration, a school does not function without its teachers, and technology in schools is minimally effective without full integration. Technology cannot be integrated without the teachers implementing technology within their classrooms. Administrators can improve technology integration not only through continuing to provide instructional leadership and support but also through building teacher capacity and leadership.

Kopcha (2012) found that ongoing PD beyond implementation, mentoring, and continued support from professional learning communities (PLCs) improved and sustained technology integration. Administrators must be intentional in bringing teachers into the conversation about technology integration and supporting them as they learn to utilize technology tools as a part of their instruction.

Ongoing PD

It is rare for technology to be successfully integrated into a school after one PD session. As with teaching students new skills, it is important to allow school personnel to have multiple opportunities to encounter new technology before they are able to use it independently. Often, the first PD session on new technology comes from district personnel (e.g., information technology staff, instructional technology team) or a software company representative.

This training introduces school personnel to the new technology and gives a fast-paced overview of how to get started. While the most tech-savvy individuals will leave the session feeling confident, many attendees will feel overwhelmed and confused by the information. If this is the one and only PD session for school personnel, it is highly unlikely that the new technology will become integrated. However, ongoing PD will allow for much better results.

If an administrator has been in a building with consistent staff for some years, they will already have an idea of who will be ready to walk out of a PD session and begin utilizing the technology in their classroom instruction (they may have already set it up while training was still happening!) and who is likely to wait to bring the technology into their classrooms until they are forced. After the first PD session, a brief survey (much like an exit ticket given to the students at the end of a lesson) can be used to identify those who will need additional support and to what extent.

Since there seems to never be enough time in the day for an educator, it is important to optimize what time is available to best support the individual needs of teachers. For those who do not need additional PD sessions and have integrated the new technology into their classroom, it is not necessary for them to receive continued PD in which they will not be learning. For those who need extensive support in learning new technology, there are creative ways to find time for them to interact with the technology without adding to their plate.

For example, think of other school staff who may be able to monitor students during noninstructional time (e.g., recess, lunch, dismissal) so that a teacher can practice using the technology with you or a peer who understands the technology well. For elementary grades, find a reading buddy classroom where one teacher can supervise as older students read with younger students, while the other teacher watches videos on how to use the technology. For secondary subjects, consider ways so that two classes can work on an activity collaboratively outdoors while one teacher focuses on using a program from a practice student account.

Whether confident or nervous about technology that has been integrated into a school, the use of newer technology will diminish over time if ongoing PD does not occur. At the beginning of each school year, spend some time during all staff meetings to discuss the technology that has been integrated into the school and give brief refreshers on how to use each tool. Again, conduct an informal survey to see who may need more to get back into the groove of using the technology purposefully in their classroom.

Throughout the school year, check to see who is utilizing the technology effectively in their classroom and who has let it fade into the distance when conducting walkthroughs. If you have an observation checklist, add the technology to it to show the value of integration. Have conversations with those who do not have the technology integrated into their instruction and find out what support they need to get back to regular and daily use.

Mentoring

Mentoring is beneficial for anyone who may be learning a new skill. School administrators are well positioned to mentor teachers within their building, as the role of school administrator includes providing support for teachers. A mentor for technology integration should check in with mentees who need additional support on a frequent basis in the beginning and less regularly as mentees gain confidence. Mentees may simply need encouragement or a connection to the vision and purpose of integrating new technology into their instruction.

Developing a relationship with a mentor alleviates stress and barriers to technology integration, while also allowing the mentor to understand where the greatest areas of need for support remain. Once the mentee feels comfortable using new technology, it is important to continue to check on them and offer them encouragement, so their use of the technology remains integrated and their anxiety does not return.

Support from PLCs

Though it is ideal to mentor numerous individual teachers, the reality is that there may not be enough time to do so. Instead, administrators should consider creating PLCs for new technology, as well as technology that has been previously integrated into the school. PLCs can be grade level or subject area teams, groups with homogeneous abilities from a variety of grade levels or subject areas, or groups with heterogeneous abilities from a variety of grade levels or subject areas. Regardless of the makeup of these PLCs, regular meetings should be scheduled for the PLCs to have discussions and provide support for one another.

If regular meetings become straining for teachers' schedules, have the group check in with each other regularly via email and have them carbon copy the administration. As a PLC, discussions can be had about what is going well, who may need support or have questions, and creative ways to integrate technology into instruction. PLCs should regularly review student data and discuss student engagement with technology. A key component of the PLC for technology integration is support for one another, whether be it about the use of the program or purely in the form of encouragement.

Distributing Leadership

While administration should remain at the head of technology integration, administration does not have to do it all alone. There are leaders across school buildings everywhere, though their leadership abilities may not always be tapped into. Administrators should think about who in their building has exceptional technological skills and leadership abilities. Spillane, Diamon, and Jita (2003) discuss distributed school leadership as incorporating multiple individuals, both formal and informal leaders, in a school who can mobilize and guide school staff through the instructional innovation process.

Technology integration is in perfect alignment with instructional innovation. To be innovative within a school, it is optimal to have multiple leaders involved. The school principal should lead the innovation but can be joined by a team made up of other school administrators, instructional coaches, classroom teachers, and other school personnel (e.g., librarian, counselors, computer lab instructor).

As previously discussed, school administration should be at the helm of technology integration, but they should also leverage the strengths of other leaders within the building. Is there a teacher who is particularly good at explaining how to use technology to others? A counselor who is great at offering encouragement and building others up? An instructional coach who is exceptional at interpreting data and communicating what that data mean? A teacher who finds innovative ways to incorporate technology into their lessons?

Invite those professionals to be part of an instructional technology team. The first teacher can help lead training on new or integrated technology; the counselor can lead breakout groups to discuss how people are feeling during training; the instructional coach can play a critical role in explaining how the school is utilizing the technology; and the other teacher can provide examples of lessons that incorporate technology in a meaningful way.

Consider the case of Bev and Elizabeth. Elizabeth was a tech-savvy classroom teacher new to Bev's school. Before the school year began, Bev, the school's principal, talked to Elizabeth about leading PD for those interested in learning more about the software suite being used across the district. Bev had attended some training but wanted to see how the software suite could be used in a more valuable way in classrooms across the school.

Elizabeth agreed to provide PD for anyone interested at the school during a teacher workday. The session was not required, but Bev specifically reached out to teachers who typically did not interface with technology meaningfully in their classrooms. Those in attendance at the session had a range of comfort and familiarity with technology generally and with the software suite. Bev was an active participant in the session and spent time learning more deeply about the software suite on her own later.

Throughout the school year, Bev and Elizabeth collaborated on subsequent PD sessions for teachers. When Elizabeth moved to a different district, Bev continued coleading PD sessions with other teachers, which allowed the software suite integration to be sustained, while Bev continued to improve professionally, distributed leadership with teachers, and improved teachers' capacity.

Communicating with Parents and the Community

With a shift to distance learning and online classwork/homework, parents are learning more about the technology that is used in their child's classroom. Thus, communicating technology integration with parents and community members who work with students (e.g., afterschool daycare staff) is more important than ever. When children can access technology outside of their classroom, it is invaluable to have the adults in their lives understand how the technology is to be used.

For example, many classrooms now use Google Classroom as a way for students to turn in assignments. Younger students may use paper and a pencil or crayons, and then take a picture of their work with the camera on their laptops/tablets to turn in online. Many teachers have students complete quizzes via Google Forms. So how do parents assist their child and also see the outcomes of student work when assignments and quizzes are not being sent home in paper form?

Schools can offer training sessions for parents and community members during times that they are likely to be available. These sessions should be recorded and made available on the school website or sent via links in emails for those who are unable to attend. If having in-person training sessions is not feasible, school personnel can record how-to videos for parents and community members to watch when they have time.

During training, school personnel should go over student expectations, discuss what technology is available and integrated, demonstrate how to complete the most important tasks, and allow parents and community members time to practice using the technology. Different grade levels and subject areas may use different technology, so it is important to be mindful of what information is necessary for all or just for some.

Consider having different sessions at different times (e.g., primary and upper elementary, different subject areas) or creating videos to be available on classroom websites. Helping parents and community members understand technology that is integrated into classrooms will not only assist students with the technology, but it can also bolster positive communication and create mutual understanding before difficult situations arise.

Finding the Best Educational Tools for Your School

There is a plethora of educational software available, and all of it claims to improve student learning and engagement better than the other programs on the market. So how can a school administrator determine what will be the best fit for their school? Be purposeful in how you select software; do not select the latest and greatest just because you have heard from many that it is wonderful. Research the proposed model utilized that is the basis for the touted increased student achievement results. Will that model work for your school? Always ask the publisher for the model and achievement gains report. Examine the data closely.

If there is a need to improve reading mastery, look specifically for options that focus on reading. If that latest and greatest improves mathematics skills, it is the wrong choice for your school. Not sure where you can get the most bang for your buck? Talk to other administrators to find out what they are using that has been successful in a school similar in demographics to yours and ask teachers if there is a program they used at another school that they felt was impactful for student learning.

When in doubt, the internet will tell you a lot about the educational software that is on the market today. A simple search will bring up many results with reviews from a variety of sources. Try searching using terms specific to the subject area you are interested in purchasing for (e.g., "best educational software for high school English students"). Be mindful that many of the results will be the actual websites for programs that are spending money to be listed higher up in a search. The best reviews come from nonprofit, research-based companies and education-related magazines rather than blogs.

Once you have identified some possible options for your school, ask for free limited versions from each company's representatives. Try before you buy is not just for clothes and cars! The educational software representatives want to build a relationship with you to convince you that their program is best for your school, so they may be willing to let you have temporary licenses for one grade level or subject area. If so, find a team willing to pilot the program with fidelity. This fidelity to the model must be considered fully.

Usually, your most tech-savvy teams will be up for the challenge. Get regular feedback from the team piloting each program; stop into classrooms while the program is being utilized to see whether the program is engaging students in or distracting them from learning, and remain in regular contact with the educational software representatives during your trial period. The funding you have is precious, so it is worth taking the time to find the right program that will remain integrated within the classrooms at your school. Progress monitor student achievement to see if the technology is netting the desired results.

Understanding the Impact of Technology Integration

In the end, all that happens in educational settings should revolve around the students and their learning. Your strategic plan should include how technology will aid in meeting your goals. If funds have been spent on technology that should be positively impacting student learning, it is the duty of school administration to verify that the implemented technology is doing its job. Once technology has been implemented, administrators must understand whether that technology has been truly integrated, meaning used on a regular or daily basis, within their schools.

Many software programs offer a variety of reports, such as time spent logged into a program and growth or improvement. This is an ideal time to apply the skillset of that instructional coach who is good at looking at data.

If technology has not been integrated, administrators need to review why the technology is being resisted (whether consciously or subconsciously) and by whom, and then revisit PD to address the gaps. If the technology is being integrated, administration needs to switch their focus to understanding the impact of the integration while maintaining PD activities as needed.

To understand the impact the integration of specific technology has made, there are multiple sources of data that the administrators can review. As mentioned, reports can be generated to review data use and growth by individual students, classrooms, grade levels or subject areas, and so forth. But these reports provide a very small snapshot of how the technology is impacting overall student learning. It is more valuable to review data that are typically used to determine student growth: formative and summative assessments, benchmarks, end-of-course/year exams, and the like.

If a school selected specific technology to improve reading instruction, how has reading achievement changed since technology *integration*, not since *implementation*? If there has been growth, whether small or large, consider what other factors may have contributed to that growth beyond the technology. Did the school follow the technology company's implementation guide and model of growth? Was the technology implemented with fidelity? Is this typical growth for this time in the school year or is it exceptional? If growth is exceptional and there are no other obvious contributing factors for seeing this growth, technology integration is serving its purpose.

POSSIBLE MODELS FOR ONGOING PD

Typically, new technology is introduced at the beginning of the school year when teacher workdays are available for training. However, ongoing PD is crucial for technology integration. Without ongoing PD, technology can quickly shift from integrated to forgotten. However, finding time for PD during the school year presents a major challenge. As goes with many aspects of education, creativity breeds solutions. Think of innovative ways to carve out time for PD and teachers will be more willing to participate than tacking it onto the end of other meetings.

At the school level, there are various models an administrator can employ. Of course, PD can take place in the traditional setting, with all instructional personnel present during a teacher workday or instead of a faculty meeting. In place of a full faculty meeting, consider offering a variety of "electives" where the faculty gets to select which of the multiple PD opportunities they would like to attend.

"Elective" choices should include additional training for the various technology integrated across the school. This provides opportunities for those who are confident with the various technologies in place to lead PD sessions, while sustaining multiple technology systems. Sessions could also be recorded by an administrator or other technology team leader and viewed at a convenient time with an incentive attached to it (e.g., administrator covering dismissal duty, jeans pass).

There are additional options if PD is being conducted for smaller groups. If an entire grade level or subject area team needs additional PD, offer the administration to join them during lesson planning to take on some of the tasks while they spend that time engaging with the technology. If a school is lucky enough to have PD funds, get roving substitutes to cover classrooms while one group at a time receives training. This is a perfect opportunity to group teachers in homogeneous ability groups to optimize PD time. Get creative in how to release teachers to learn technology without adding more time to their workday. Of course, PLCs are a great avenue for PD.

Opportunities for ongoing PD also exist beyond one school building. If there are multiple schools within your district that use the same technology, consider working collaboratively to provide PD sessions. These may be via a video-conferencing platform or hosted at each of the schools at different times. Consider teaming with other administrators, even those in areas farther away, to create a series of online modules for teachers to work through.

District-level PD can also occur. A large district in South Carolina offers a summer institute where teachers and administrators propose sessions, and educators from across the district select which sessions they would like to attend for continuing education credits. A large district in California offers teachers half-day PD sessions where they can request a substitute in order to attend the training at the district office. If your district does not currently have any districtwide PD offerings, consider proposing this to your district administration as a way to increase teacher capacity and, therefore, improve student learning outcomes.

SUMMARY

Technology can be a key component in enhancing student learning, especially as technology has become more accessible across the country. While there is an abundance of challenges administrators face when attempting to implement and integrate technology, there are numerous creative solutions. Administrators must remain at the forefront of technology integration, though they should think about the leaders around the school whose skills and abilities would be an asset to an instructional technology team.

Educational and instructional leaders must identify the best educational tools for their schools and understand the impact of those tools to ensure that the technology aids, not distracts, learning in classrooms. Administrators must continue to improve professionally with technology to improve teachers' capacity with technology, provide opportunities for ongoing professional develop and support for school personnel, and communicate with parents and the community. School administrators play a critical role in technology's impact on student learning outcomes.

REFLECTION QUESTIONS

1. Think about the technology within your own school building. Take a moment to jot down answers to the following questions:
   a. What technology has been truly integrated, meaning used on a daily/routine basis?
   b. What has been integrated by some successfully but is not used widely around the building?
   c. What is available to your school but is not being utilized?
   d. What systems are you aware of that you would like to integrate at your school?

   Now, refer to the chapter and write down some ideas you may be willing to try to improve technology within your school.

2. Who are the tech-savvy individuals in your district and/or building? How can they help your school with technology integration?
3. What would make you and others at your school feel more confident about technology integration? What resources might be available to build that confidence?
4. Write down your strengths with technology, as an individual and as a PLC. How can you leverage these strengths to improve student outcomes across your school?
5. Discuss Kopcha's (2012) five barriers to technology integration in relationship to your school. What barriers exist and what are the plans to remove them?

REFERENCES

Hallinger, P. (2010). Developing instructional leadership. In B. Davies & M. Brundrett (Eds.), *Developing Successful Leadership*, pp. 61–76. Studies in Educational Leadership (Vol. 11). Springer. https://doi.org/10.1007/978-90-481-9106-2_5

Howard, S. K. (2013). Risk-aversion: Understanding teachers' resistance to technology integration. *Technology, Pedagogy and Education, 22*(3), 357–72. https://doi.org/10.1080/1475939X.2013.802995

Kopcha, T. J. (2012). Teachers' perceptions of the barriers to technology integration and practices with technology under situated professional development. *Computers & Education, 59*(4), 1109–21. https://doi.org/10.1016/j.compedu.2012.05.014

National Forum on Education Statistics. (2002). *Technology in schools: Suggestions, tools and guidelines for assessing technology in elementary and secondary education* (Report No. 2003313). National Center for Education Statistics. https://nces.ed.gov/pubsearch/pubsinfo.asp?pubid=2003313

Southworth, G. (2010). Instructional leadership in schools: Reflections and empirical evidence. *School Leadership & Management, 22*(1), 73–91. https://doi.org/10.1080/13632430220143042

Spillane, J. P., Diamon, J. B., & Jita, L. (2003). The distribution of leadership for instruction. *Journal of Curriculum Studies, 35*(5), 533–43. https://doi.org/10.1080/0022027021000041972

Chapter Five

The Importance of School Law for the School Leader

Kent Murray, The Citadel

With litigation in public schools at an all-time high and ever increasing, the need for school principals and district leaders to have a comprehensive understanding of existing law and educational policy is more important than ever. Students in programs for school leadership must develop an understanding of legal issues, the ability to research existing law and interpret their findings for those they lead, and maintain compliance with existing school board policy regulations.

Principals must address traditional and novel legal issues in their schools daily as they walk the fine line of maintaining the appropriate decorum of the learning environment while ensuring the protection of student rights and responsibilities. To be an effective school leader in the legal arena, school leaders must develop and maintain a current understanding of school law through the five fundamental school law principles for school leaders.

FUNDAMENTAL SCHOOL LAW PRINCIPLES FOR SCHOOL LEADERS

1. School law is constantly evolving and changing.
2. School leaders must understand the value of legal advice and the importance of partnering with school district legal counsel to ensure compliance with the law.
3. School leaders must remain vigilant in their commitment to communicate with district leaders and legal counsel when encountering novel legal questions and decisions.
4. School board policy is the required rule book of school law for school leaders.

5. School leaders are the responsible party for providing professional development on school legal issues to those they lead.

SCHOOL LAW IS CONSTANTLY EVOLVING AND CHANGING

For many decades, public schools in the United States have served as a laboratory for social and legal issues such as racial integration (*Brown v. Board of Education of Topeka*, 1954; *Mendez et al. v. Westminster School District of Orange County et al.*, 1947), speech and expression rights of public school students (*Tinker v. Des Moines Independent Community School District*, 1969), and the rights of students with special needs (Education of All Handicapped Children Act, Public Law 94–142, 1975).

More recently, the role of public schools in the development of legal precedent regarding student rights continues, with the courts focusing on transgender student rights (*G.G. v. Gloucester County School Board*, 2020) and the authority of school leadership to regulate off-campus social media speech (*Mahanoy Area School District v. B.L.*, 2021). School leaders must accept and adapt as the landscape of school law continues to evolve regarding legal issues in K–12 schools.

To be effective leaders, school administrators must maintain a current understanding of the pending and decided case laws. Case law, also known as common law, is based on precedent from decisions made by the courts regarding a particular case. For the purpose of this chapter, *New Jersey v. T.L.O.* (1985) will be the example of case law and how it impacts the duties of school leadership, decisions made by school leaders, school board policy, and administrative regulations (ARs) to be discussed later in the chapter.

The importance of case law can be found in the legal doctrine stare decisis, a Latin term for "let the decision stand" (*Black's Law Dictionary*, 2022). The principle requires judges to be bound by previous decisions of the court when deciding a legal matter. For school leaders, case law provides a current understanding of the legal decisions that assist administrators when dealing with a matter having the potential to infringe upon student rights under the law.

Aspiring school leaders should develop the skills to interpret case law to understand the facts of the case, legal questions being considered by the court, the decision of the court, and an understanding of the opinions written by the judges to fully understand the rationale behind the decision. The facts of the case describe specifically the scenario being adjudicated by the court. To assist in understanding the court decisions, school leaders should utilize an online law dictionary, such as *Black's Law Dictionary* (https://thelawdictionary.org/), to interpret any legal language found in the published opinion of the court. **Assignment**: To further understand the importance of a legal dictionary, search online for the legal doctrine of in loco parentis. This concept adopted by the U.S. court system from English common law is a founding principle of American school law defining the supervision relationship and authority between educators and their students.

In essence, one must question the events and actions of the situation and decision being challenged legally. The facts of the case for *T.L.O.* would be any pertinent information regarding the search and seizure of the fourteen-year-old student by school officials. Following the lawsuit from the student against the school district, the court answered legal questions involving the actions of school officials searching a public school student.

The judge's decision and the rationale given provided the court's decision and opinion to the matter being litigated. As will be discussed later in the chapter, the court made the decision in this case that the public school students do have privacy rights; so, school officials must meet the standard of reasonable suspicion prior to conducting a search. The ramifications of this case are far-reaching in all school settings.

School leaders must continuously review recent case law and interpret these decisions for those they lead to ensure compliance with their precedent. This can be accomplished by remaining current on new legal issues and decisions. Professional development opportunities can be accessed through school district workshops, legal workshops through state school boards associations, mentoring and guidance from school district legal counsel, and obtaining a membership in an organization that provides school law information.

The Education Law Association (https://www.educationlaw.org/) is the premiere organization for educators to remain updated on recent and pending legal decisions in school law. The organization offers many professional development opportunities for school leaders, including a monthly ED LAW Update, subscription to digital periodicals, e-newsletter, the Yearbook of Education Law, annual conferences, and workshops. With an annual subscription, educators can receive a wealth of information necessary to remain well versed on pending and decided school law issues.

SCHOOL LEADERS MUST UNDERSTAND THE VALUE OF LEGAL ADVICE AND THE IMPORTANCE OF PARTNERING WITH SCHOOL DISTRICT LAWYERS TO ENSURE COMPLIANCE WITH THE EVER-CHANGING LAW

School leaders must possess and maintain a high level of legal knowledge as they lead their fellow educators in dealing with a myriad of old and new school law issues. It is imperative that they remain current on new legal precedent and continue their mastery of existing school law. To do so, school leaders must develop a relationship with district legal counsel and trust their opinions, especially when faced with a novel issue. Legal counsel provides the school leader with the appropriate response when dealing with potential or pending litigation. As such, school attorneys are most important when a new legal question is considered by the courts.

Looking through the eyes of a fellow school leader involved in what would become a landmark Supreme Court case is an excellent opportunity for aspiring school leaders to understand the importance of legal counsel for potential or pending litigation. Consider the story of Assistant Vice Principal Theodore Choplick of Piscataway High School in Middlesex County, New Jersey, in the Supreme Court decision, *New Jersey v. T.L.O.*

On March 4, 1980, a teacher at the high school discovered two female students smoking cigarettes in the high school student restroom. The teacher escorted both students to the principal's office where they met with Vice Principal Choplick to discuss the smoking allegation. While one student admitted to the misconduct, fourteen-year-old T.L.O. denied smoking in the restroom and went as far as to notify the vice principal she did not smoke cigarettes.

Following the student's denial, the vice principal faced a school law decision based upon the teacher's eyewitness statement as whether to search the student's belongings to determine if she was in possession of the contraband cigarettes. At that time, there was no definitive decision from the courts on the authority of school officials to search student belongings, so Choplick made the decision to search the student based on a long-standing practice that school administrators had the authority to search if they reasonably suspect that the student was in possession of contraband.

The vice principal made the decision to search T.L.O.'s purse where he found cigarettes, marijuana, small bags used for distribution, a large amount of money, and a written communication indicating the student was selling marijuana at school. T.L.O. had not only lied about the cigarettes, but she was also found to be involved in the distribution of illegal narcotics at school.

Based on their belief that their daughter's rights had been violated against unreasonable search and seizure under the Fourth Amendment, T.L.O.'s parents made the decision to file a lawsuit against the school district. After almost five years of litigation through both state and federal courts, the Supreme Court on January 15, 1985, held in a 6–3 ruling that the search by Choplick was constitutional as it met the standard of reasonableness to conduct a student search.

The court held that the Fourth Amendment prohibition of unreasonable searches and seizure does apply to school officials as a student has a legitimate expectation of privacy; however, in this case, the search was reasonable as Choplick had established reasonable suspicion based upon the teacher's eyewitness testimony that T.L.O. was in possession of contraband in violation of school rules. The importance of this legal decision for school leaders is the establishment of reasonable suspicion, a legal standard required for school officials to apply when facing the possibility of a potential student search.

School board policy must comply with the state and federal statutory law but is also a product of case law as seen in the sample board policy provided later in the chapter. When legal decisions are rendered by the court, school officials in consultation with the legal counsel begin the process of amending or adding to the existing policy. Legal counsel will meet with school district officials to develop a policy to be considered for adoption by the school board.

Once the new or amended policy is adopted by the board, school district officials develop ARs to comply with the new legal decision. ARs provide school leaders with the expectations, process, and procedures to follow when dealing with issues regarding student rights. An example of the impact of case law on school board policy and ARs will follow later in the chapter by examining a school board policy and ARs for student search and seizure.

New Jersey v. T.L.O. is an excellent example of how a case law impacts the duties of the school officials. This decision established a standard of reasonableness for school officials when conducting searches by requiring any student search to be justified at its inception by reasonable suspicion. Administrators are not held to the more difficult standard of probable cause as required by law enforcement nor is a search warrant required. School officials are required to meet the two-part legal test established by the court: first, the search must be justified by reasonable suspicion at its inception, and, second, the scope of the search must be reasonably related to the circumstances of the incident (*New Jersey v. T.L.O.*, 1985).

SCHOOL LEADERS MUST REMAIN VIGILANT IN THEIR COMMITMENT TO COMMUNICATE WITH DISTRICT LEADERS AND LEGAL COUNSEL WHEN ENCOUNTERING NOVEL LEGAL QUESTIONS AND DECISIONS

Because of the nature of schools and its entanglement with societal issues and the legal requirement to protect student rights, school leaders face novel legal issues daily. Many of these issues have not been experienced before or there may not be an existing definitive decision from the courts for school leaders to follow. Because of this, school leaders must be vigilant in their communication with district officials and act with good faith when experiencing a novel legal issue.

Courts are consistent in invoking good faith when school officials act in a reasonable, good faith manner, despite later changes in the law. Communication with legal counsel in all legal matters is paramount in ensuring the protection of student rights and school districts. As the old school community relations maxim reminds school leaders, elementary students love surprises, superintendents and school boards do not.

School districts may receive their legal advice via in-house counsel and/or outside counsel. The main difference between the two resides in the following: in-house counsel is an employee of the school district and works full time within the school district dealing with daily legal issues and managing the use of outside counsel when necessary for outsourced legal matters.

School leaders with legal questions or issues work more frequently through their district leadership and in-house counsel as outside counsel is typically used for novel and larger legal matters. An effective partnership and communication with legal counsel and district leadership when dealing with school legal issues is paramount.

SCHOOL BOARD POLICY IS THE REQUIRED RULE BOOK OF SCHOOL LAW FOR SCHOOL LEADERS

The most important legal document for school leaders in any school district is the school board policy manual. The board policy manual is a set of policies and ARs that reflect the expectation of the school board for school leaders when dealing with school issues. This manual is the product of decades of evolution to ensure that the school board policy and procedures are compliant with changes in the state and federal statutory law, as well as new decisions in case law.

Simply stated, the board policy manual is a practical rule book for school administrators that clearly outline the expectations of school district leadership in their role of enforcing the expectations of the school board. A violation of school board policy is the most frequent reason for the termination of school leaders. As school districts continue to experience crippling litigation fees across the country, it is imperative that school leaders protect their school district assets and revenue by ensuring compliance with existing law and its requirements.

A school board policy consists of describing the purpose and intent of the policy, the legal requirements for its existence, and direction for the particular policy topic. School boards, through the advice of legal counsel, review and approve board policy with the expectation this policy will be enforced by the board's chief executive officer, the superintendent. While the board is responsible for the development of policy, it is the superintendent that develops the procedures, known as ARs, to provide guidance for school leaders on how to properly carry out their duties under that particular policy.

A current example of school board policy and ARs for student search and seizure are provided for review later in the chapter. The legal responsibility for public education was granted to state legislatures via the Tenth Amendment's Reserved Powers Clause created from the following language: "The powers not delegated to the United States by the Constitution, nor prohibited by it to the states, are reserved to the states respectively, or to the people" (U.S. Const. amend. X.).

Because public education was not identified in the U.S. Constitution as a responsibility of the federal government, public education was delegated to the state legislatures to determine how to operate their public schools. States, in turn, provided plenary authority through state statutes to local school boards to ensure local control of the operation of schools. Aspiring school principals must familiarize themselves with local school board policy as policy guides decision-making on all education matters.

School board policy is intended to provide guidance for effectively operating the school district; guide school staff in carrying out their duties; promote progress toward the school district's goals, mission, and the necessary information and procedures for educators to carry out the duties for which they have been employed. School board policy is the "rule book" for educators.

School board authority does have limitations as it must be compliant with state and federal constitutional provisions, state and federal legislative enactments, state board of education rules and regulations, legal interpretation and opinions, and demands of constituents as schools are governed by the community through their elected board members who serve as the representative of voters.

Policy development is the responsibility of the school board with guidance from legal counsel, but the superintendent and district office leadership determine the procedures required of school officials, known as ARs. An AR provides educators with the specific procedural steps for complying with a school board policy. District leaders use ARs to provide school leaders and educators with specific actions to be carried out or limit pathways of response.

Board policy is the school leader's friend and intended to provide procedural safeguards in their handling of student issues. In an effort to better understand the requirements of board policy, JCAB Students Searches, Student Interrogations and Arrests assume that you are serving as a high school assistant principal who has just been notified that a local law enforcement agent is at your school to question a student regarding an issue in the community. Board policy provides you with the required procedures to follow. Per policy JCAB, you must cooperate with law enforcement and request to be present during the discussion as long as your presence does not impede the investigation. Any questioning should take place in a private area. Your responsibility to the student and their parent/guardian is to make a reasonable attempt to contact them and request that they be present during the questioning and, if you are unable to connect, continue making a reasonable attempt to contact and notify them that the law enforcement questioning took place. A school leader that complies with board policy and ARs is acting in good faith in their role as a school leader.

School board policy manuals are organized into separate chapters based upon the topic the policy is addressing. Students in educational leadership programs should continuously review their board policy to ensure understanding of the purpose of the policy and the ARs required for school employees. Most school boards use a software program titled Board Docs (https://boarddocs.com/), created specifically for boards of education to manage documents, board policy, and to provide transparency to stakeholders.

Aspiring school leaders are encouraged to review their school board's policy manual and to learn how to navigate through board policy and other documents through this software platform. An example of the organization of a board policy manual is given below:

BCSD Policy Manual Organization

- A. Foundations and Basic Commitments
- B. Board Government and Operations
- C. General School Administration
- D. Fiscal Management
- E. Business Management
- F. Facilities Management Program
- G. Personnel
- I. Instructional Program
- J. Students
- K. School Community Home Relations

(Berkeley County School District, n.d.)

Case law is based on precedent from decisions made by the courts regarding a particular case. A great example of the impact of case law on board policy can be found in the Supreme Court decision in *New Jersey v. T.L.O.*, where the U.S. Supreme Court provided specific procedures for school leaders who conduct searches on students.

In the case study, aspiring school leaders are required to review a sample school board policy and ARs, titled JCAB Students Searches, Student Interrogations and Arrests and the associated ARs (Policy) and AR JCAB-R Searches, Student Interrogations and Arrests (AR). This policy and the procedures in the ARs are based on this landmark U.S. Supreme Court decision and legal counsel to ensure compliance with the law and protections of a student's Fourth Amendment rights.

SCHOOL LEADERS ARE THE RESPONSIBLE PARTY FOR PROVIDING PROFESSIONAL DEVELOPMENT ON SCHOOL LEGAL ISSUES TO THOSE THEY LEAD

The principal is the instructional leader of the school and has the ultimate responsibility for the professional development of those they lead. A large amount of litigation in the field of school law is based upon the supervision of students by their teachers and school leaders. Educators are provided with the authority of in loco parentis as they serve in the place of the parent when supervising their children during school hours. Educators have a portion of the powers of the parent as is necessary to fulfill the duties for which they have been employed. Because educators make decisions daily on legal issues in their classrooms and when supervising children, school leaders must plan professional development and implement procedures to ensure that student rights and responsibilities are not infringed upon and school districts are spared from costly litigation.

Professional Development Tips for School Leaders

1. *Faculty Meeting School Board Policy Updates*—Consider reviewing one board policy at each scheduled faculty meeting. Select a policy that directly impacts the classroom, student discipline, supervision of students, or other policies that directly impact faculty and staff.
2. *Weekly/Monthly School Board Policy Spotlight via Weekly Communication*—Consider including board policy updates in your communication with faculty and staff.
3. *School Law Publication*—Consider using a publication from a reputable source to provide targeted professional development for educators. For guidelines for educators on the topic of religious issues in schools such as prayer or the use of the bible, consider using a document from the Freedom from the Religious Freedom Center titled *A Teacher's Guide to Religion in the Public Schools* (Haynes, 2004). Examples of questions and

answers on many topics faced by educators include the topic of teachers expressing their religious views while at school, "May I pray or otherwise practice my faith while at school?" (Haynes, 2004, pg. 6) and the topic of students expressing their religious views, "May students express religious views in public schools?" (pg. 7).

4. *Department Head Meetings*—Consider these meetings as another avenue to share updated information with faculty so that they can conduct mini professional development in department meetings.
5. *Leadership Team Meetings*—Consider sharing updates and practice, applying the principles to school-specific scenarios. The expectation is that the leadership team helps to support teachers across all disciplines. These practice sessions may result in a change in school procedures.
6. *Human Resource Training*—School district must provide educators with continuous professional development through training, workshops, and video modules. School leaders must emphasize these necessary training opportunities to provide teachers with the expectations of school district leadership in areas such as the requirement of educators to protect student records as required by the Family Educational Rights and Privacy Act (FERPA, 1974) or sexual harassment in the workforce. These training videos are developed with legal assistance and are intended to eliminate illegal practices.

SCHOOL LAW CASE STUDY

In an effort to understand the connection between school law and its impact on board policy and ARs, this case study will provide the opportunity for an aspiring school leader to respond to a simulation involving a current school leader facing a potential student search and seizure. Utilizing your understanding of the U.S. Supreme Court decision of *New Jersey v. T.L.O.*, a current board policy titled JCAB Students Searches, Student Interrogations and Arrests and AR titled, AR JCAB-R Searches, Student Interrogations and Arrests respond to the questions listed below.

Aspiring school leaders are encouraged to secure the school board policy manual for their own school district to locate their district's specific policy and ARs required of school officials when conducting a potential student search. This enables the student to practice navigating their own board policy manual while determining any differences in the language of the policy or required procedural steps from the policy below. Using the sample board policy and ARs provided below, answer the following questions based upon your understanding of the board policy requirements.

CASE STUDY: TO SEARCH OR NOT TO SEARCH—THAT IS THE QUESTION

You are serving as an assistant principal at Carson High School. After returning from the bus loop at the beginning of the school day, you are notified by social studies teacher Jason Powell that a student in his homeroom notified him that another student on the bus sitting next to the reporter showed him a small bag of marijuana and attempted to sell the illegal contraband. The reporting student positively identified the student as Brent Simmons. The teacher reported that he asked several questions to the student accuser to determine the accuracy of the allegation.

The student provided definitive information, including the name of the student, where the student was hiding the bag of marijuana in his bookbag, and a description of the amount in the bag. Both you and the teacher know the student accuser and believe he is providing an honest representation of the events on the bus. Utilizing the sample school board policy below, **JCAB Students Searches, Student Interrogations and Arrests** and the associated ARs, **AR JCAB-R Searches, Student Interrogations and Arrests**, answer the following questions.

1. Will you conduct a search of the student and their belongings?
2. What standard of proof is required to search a public school student? Do you have the required standard of proof?
3. Per the ARs, what are the specific steps you will follow if you decide to conduct a search? If so, what are the specific requirements from the policy to conduct this search?
4. If you find illegal drugs on the student, you are required by state statutory law to contact law enforcement. What specific actions will you take when contacting law enforcement?
5. If law enforcement interrogates and/or arrests the students, what does the policy require you to do?
6. What are the sources of law used to develop this policy?

SUMMARY

As the increase in litigation in public schools continues amid the debilitating costs for school districts, the role of a school leader must evolve and adapt to one with a current knowledge of existing and pending legal issues in an era of constant change. School leaders must learn to be effective partners with district administration and legal counsel to ensure effective compliance with existing case law and policy issues.

For today's principal to be effective in our litigious society, school leaders must provide professional development on legal issues and school board policy to ensure compliance with existing law and precedence. School-based educators are on the front line of school law issues and must develop relationships with effective communication with district leaders and counsel. School leaders are held accountable for assisting their school districts to avoid potential litigation by making sound decisions based on established policy and procedures. To be effective, school leaders must maintain and promote to those they lead a current understanding of law by utilizing the five fundamental school law principles found in this chapter.

SAMPLE SCHOOL BOARD POLICY AND ARS FOR CASE STUDY JCAB STUDENTS SEARCHES, STUDENT INTERROGATIONS AND ARRESTS

Adopted December 1, 1993
Last Revised February 24, 2004
The board by this policy recognizes that both state law and the Fourth Amendment to the U.S. Constitution protect citizens, including students, from unreasonable searches and seizures. The board accordingly directs all district personnel to conduct searches and seizures on district property or during district-sponsored events in accordance with applicable federal and state laws. The board's express intention for this policy is to enhance security in the schools, prevent students and other persons on school grounds from violating board policies, school rules and state and federal laws, and to ensure that legitimate privacy interests and expectations are respected, consistent with the need of the district to maintain a safe environment conducive to education.

SEARCHES

As authorized by state law, district and school administrators and officials may conduct reasonable searches on district property of lockers; desks; vehicles; and personal belongings, such as purses, book bags, wallets and satchels, with or without probable cause, subject to the limitations and requirements of this policy.

The district administration is directed to ensure compliance with S.C. Code Ann. § 59–63–1150, which requires that administrators must receive training in the "reasonableness standard" under existing law and in district procedures regarding searches. The district administration is further authorized and directed to establish procedures to be followed in conducting searches. The board further directs the district administration to ensure that notice is posted in compliance with S.C. Code Ann. § 59-63-1160 advising that any person entering the premises of any school in the district will be deemed to have consented to a reasonable search of his or her person and effects.

All searches must comply fully with the "reasonableness standard" set forth in *New Jersey v. T.L.O.*, 469 U.S. 328 (1985). This reasonableness standard recognizes that balancing the privacy interests of students with the substantial need of teachers and administrators to maintain order in the schools does not require that searches be based on the probable cause to believe that the subject of the search has violated or is violating the law. Rather, the appropriateness of a search depends on the reasonableness, under all the circumstances, of the search. Determining the reasonableness of any search will involve a twofold inquiry. First, a district or school administrator or official must determine that the search is justified at its inception, and second, that the scope and conduct of the search is reasonably related to the circumstances justifying the search at its inception. In other words, all searches hereunder must be determined to: (1) have reasonable grounds for suspecting that the search will disclose evidence that the student, or other person, has violated or is violating either the law or the rules of the district or school; and (2) be limited in scope and conduct to the extent that the measures utilized to carry out the search are reasonably related to the objectives of the search and not excessively intrusive in light of the age and sex of the person searched and the nature of the suspected infraction of the law or district or school rules.

The board further prohibits any district employee, including district administrators and officials, from conducting a strip search.

Searches involving the use of metal detectors will be conducted in accordance with the procedures outlined in policy JCAC and administrative rule JCAC-R.

Any contraband items or evidence of a violation of law or district or school rules may be retained by school officials and/or turned over to an appropriate law enforcement agency, as required by law.

CONTACTING LAW ENFORCEMENT

As required by S.C. Code Ann. § 59-24-60, school administrators will contact law enforcement immediately upon notice that a person is engaging, or has engaged, in activities on school property or at a school sanctioned or sponsored activity, which may result, or result, in injury or serious threat of injury to the person, another person or his or her property. Such reportable activities or conduct may include, but are not limited to, the examples of criminal conduct referenced in Level III of board policy JCDA (Student Behavior Code).

The board recognizes that, when law enforcement authorities are contacted pursuant to S.C. Code Ann. § 59-24-60, the law enforcement authorities must make the determination whether they will conduct an investigation into the matter. If the law enforcement authorities determine an investigation is appropriate, school officials will make reasonable efforts to discuss the scope and methods of the investigation with the law enforcement authorities as they affect school operations in an effort to minimize any disruption to the school and its students.

School officials may contact law enforcement authorities for assistance in addressing concerns other than those which must be reported pursuant to § 59-24-60. In such circumstances, the principal or his or her designee will confer with the superintendent or his or her designee prior to involving law enforcement authorities, other than a school resource officer. The superintendent or his or her designee will consult with appropriate school officials and law enforcement authorities to determine that the proposed involvement and methods of law enforcement are reasonable and consistent with this policy and will have a minimally disruptive effect on school operations and student rights.

INTERROGATIONS BY SCHOOL PERSONNEL AND SCHOOL RESOURCE OFFICERS

Administrators and teachers, as well as school resource officers, may question students about any matter pertaining to the operation of a school and/or enforcement of its rules. The questioning will be conducted discreetly and under circumstances that will avoid, to the extent practical under the circumstances, unnecessary embarrassment to the person being questioned. School resource officers will act consistently with law enforcement guidelines should any routine questioning turn into a criminal investigation. Any student who answers falsely or evasively or who refuses to answer an appropriate question may be disciplined.

INTERROGATIONS BY LAW ENFORCEMENT

When law enforcement officers find it necessary to question a student during the school day regarding matters not connected to the school, the principal or his or her designee will cooperate with law enforcement and will request to be present, so long as his or her presence does not impede the investigation. The principal or his or her designee should make a reasonable attempt to contact the student's parent/legal guardian and request his or her presence. Should this attempt fail, the principal or his or her designee will continue to make a reasonable attempt to notify the student's parent/legal guardian that law enforcement questioning took place on school grounds. However, school officials will not act in such a manner that will interfere with an ongoing law enforcement investigation. Additionally, normal visitor's protocol must be followed by law enforcement officials at all times.

Interrogations of students by law enforcement officials should generally take place in a private area, whether or not the principal or his/her designee is present.

CUSTODY OR ARREST

Law enforcement authorities have the right to enter the school to take a student into custody or to make a lawful arrest of a student, provided that they act pursuant to lawful procedure. If a student is arrested or taken into custody at school, school officials will make a reasonable effort to notify the parents/legal guardians immediately.

Adopted 7/28/92; Revised 11/93, 2/24/04
Legal references:
U.S. Supreme Court Cases:
New Jersey v. T.L.O., 469 U.S. 328 (1985).
S.C. Code of Laws
Section 59-24-60—Requires administrators to contact law enforcement.
Section 59-63-1110 et seq.—Search of persons and effects on school property.
(JCAB Students Searches, Student Interrogations and Arrests, Issued February 2004, Berkeley County School District (SC) Board of Education School Board Policy Manual. Retrieved January 30, 2022, from https://go.boarddocs.com/sc/berkeley/Board.nsf/Public#.)

AR JCAB-R SEARCHES, STUDENT INTERROGATIONS, AND ARRESTS

Issued 2/04

In order to recognize and protect student rights and expectations to privacy, safety, and an educational environment conducive to learning, as well as to enhance security in schools and prevent students from violating board policies, school rules and federal and state laws, district officials, including principals and their designees, are authorized to conduct reasonable searches according to the procedures outlined herein and in board policy JCAB.

If a search yields evidence that a board policy, school rule, or federal or state law has been violated, appropriate disciplinary action will be taken and in cases where the evidence suggests conduct which must be reported to law enforcement under S.C. Code Ann. § 59-24-60, the appropriate law enforcement authorities will be immediately notified.

SEARCHES OF A PERSON OR A PERSON'S BELONGINGS OR EFFECTS

Procedures for searching a person or a person's belongings must be reasonable. A reasonable search is one that is both based on a reasonable suspicion and reasonably related in scope. For reasonable suspicion to exist, school officials conducting a search must be able to articulate why, based on all the circumstances, they objectively and reasonably suspect the search of the person or personal property is likely to yield evidence of a violation of law, district rules, or school rules. In formulating a reasonable suspicion, a school official may rely on information he or she considers reliable, including reports from students, as well as the official's own observations, knowledge, and experience; however, a mere hunch or guess that a search will uncover evidence of a violation of law, district, or school rules is insufficient to justify a search.

Additionally, the search must be reasonable in its method and scope. A search must be carried out in such a manner that it targets the object of the search or the suspected evidence of a violation of law, district rules, or school rules. The proper scope of the search is a case-by-case determination and is generally limited to the places in which it is reasonably suspected that the object of the search may be found. A search may be as extensive as is reasonably required to locate the object(s) of the search and may extend to all areas, containers, and personal effects in which the object of the search may be found. In addition, when determining the reasonableness of the scope and manner of a search, the school officials must take into account the age, sex, and other special circumstances concerning the object of the search and the person involved, as well as the nature of the suspected infraction. Should the school official determine that a pat-down search is necessary, the school official, who must be the same sex as the person searched, will escort the person to a private area to conduct the pat-down search. A witness must be present during all such searches. If a student refuses to comply, the student's parent/legal guardian and/or the police will be contacted. Under no circumstances, however, is a strip search by a school official permitted.

SEARCHES OF LOCKERS, DESKS, AND OTHER SCHOOL PROPERTY

The district provides lockers, desks, and other school property to students for their use. Because the district retains ownership of this property, school officials may conduct searches of such property, including random and unannounced searches, with or without reasonable suspicion, when such search is determined by school officials to be otherwise reasonable in light of the needs of the school. However, objects belonging to students contained in such school property will not be opened or searched except as provided in the section above. Students will be notified expressly in writing in the student handbook that such school property may be searched at any time. In conducting searches of school property, student property will be respected and not damaged.

(JCAB-R Searches, Student Interrogations and Arrests, Issued February 2004, Berkeley County School District (SC) Board of Education School Board Policy Manual. Retrieved January 30, 2022 from https://go.boarddocs.com/sc/berkeley/Board.nsf/Public#)

REFLECTION QUESTIONS

1. How does the school board policy manual impact the decisions made in the position of school principal?
2. Why is it important for school leaders to emphasize faculty and staff professional development on school policy and law?
3. How do school leaders remain current with legal precedent from case law?
4. What are the best leadership practices to emphasize to school faculty and staff the importance of their maintaining knowledge of school board policy and ARs?

REFERENCES

Berkeley County School District (n.d.). BoardDocs. Retrieved from https:// go.board-docs.com/sc/berkeley/Board.nsf/goto?open&id=C8CJDM4CA737.

Black's Law Dictionary. Retrieved January 15, 2022 from https://thelawdictionary .org/?s=stare+decisis.

BoardDocs School Board Meeting Management Software. Retrieved January 10, 2022 from https://boarddocs.com/.

Brown v. Board of Education of Topeka, 347 U.S. 483 (1954). Retrieved from https:// www.oyez.org/cases/1940-1955/347us483.

Education of All Handicapped Children Act, Pub. L. No. 94–142, 89 Stat. 773 (1975). Retrieved from https://sites.ed.gov/idea/IDEA-History.

Education Law Association, Retrieved January 15, 2022 from https://www.educationlaw.org/.

Family Educational Rights and Privacy Act (FERPA) (20 U.S.C. § 1232g; 34 CFR Part 99). Retrieved from https://www2.ed.gov/policy/gen/guid/fpco/ferpa/index .html.

G.G. v. Gloucester County School Board, 972 F.3d 586 (4th Cir. 2020). Retrieved from https://www.oyez.org/cases/2016/16-273.

Haynes, Charles (2004). *A Teacher's Guide to Religion in the Public Schools.* Nashville: Freedom Forum.

Institute First Amendment Center, Retrieved January 15, 2022 from https://www .academia.edu/5038397/TEACHERS_GUIDE_TO_RELIGION_IN_PUBLIC _SCHOOLS.

JCAB Students Searches, Student Interrogations and Arrests, Issued February 2004, Berkeley County School District (SC) Board of Education School Board Policy Manual. Retrieved January 30, 2022 from https://go.boarddocs.com/sc/berkeley/ Board.nsf/Public#.

JCAB-R Searches, Student Interrogations and Arrests, Issued February 2004, Berkeley County School District (SC) Board of Education School Board Policy Manual. Retrieved January 30, 2022 from https://go.boarddocs.com/sc/berkeley/Board.nsf/ Public#.

Mahanoy Area School District v. B.L., 141 S.Ct. 2038 (2021). Retrieved from https://www.supremeCourt.gov/opinions/20pdf/20-255_g3bi.pdf

Mendez, et al. v. Westminster School District of Orange County et al., 64 F.Supp. 544 m aff'd, 161 F.2d 774 (1947). Retrieved from https://law.justia.com/cases/federal/appellateCourts/F2/161/774/1566460/.

New Jersey v. T.L.O., 469 U.S. 325 (1985). Retrieved from https://www.law.cornell.edu/supremeCourt/text/469/325.

Tinker v. Des Moines Independent Community School District, 393 U.S. 503 (1969). Retrieved from https://www.law.cornell.edu/supremeCourt/text/393/503.

U.S. Const. amend. X. Retrieved from https://constitution.findlaw.com/amendment10.html.

Chapter Six

Principals and Special Education
What's the Big IDEA?

Amanda Stefanski, Christine LeBlanc, and Brennan Davis, Columbia College

INTRODUCTION

Over the past four decades, federal legislation and individual state requirements have prompted enormous growth in the inclusion of students with special needs in the general education classroom. When the Education for All Handicapped Children Act (EHA) was passed in 1975, it was considered landmark legislation, articulating a "compelling . . . mission to improve access to education for children with disabilities" (U.S. Department of Education, n.d., p. 3).

EHA was reauthorized in 1990 as the Individuals with Disabilities Education Act (IDEA), and the additional amendments identified in 1997 and 2004 made even more explicit the requirements for including and accommodating students with disabilities. IDEA (2004), for example, amended the principle of least restrictive environment (LRE) so that students with disabilities were included in general education classrooms to the maximum extent appropriate.

The 2004 reauthorization also included funds to provide academic and behavioral supports to those students who do not receive special education services by way of the response to intervention (RTI) model, a multitiered system of supports. RTI establishes a schoolwide initiative to support the success of all students, regardless of ability, and the principal's role is emphasized in the literature as the cornerstone for RTI efficacy (Brendle, 2015).

Principals are involved with various phases of special education programming, from the student referral process to individualized education program (IEP) implementation. Multiple researchers have established that principals make administrative decisions as it relates special education based on their experience and understanding (Sumbera, Pazey, & Lashley, 2014). It has been fifteen years since IDEA's (2004) reauthorization, and school leaders continue to report that they lack the knowledge and skills to effectively oversee their special education programs (Williams, 2015).

While this growth in special education and related principal responsibilities took place, accompanying principal preparation over the same time period was lacking. IDEA (2004) addressed this by reiterating the importance of training principals in special education oversight, but most states continue to certify principals with, at most, a single course related to students with disabilities (Brunner & Bateman, 2020; Samuels, 2018).

This gap highlights the need for professional development as well, given that the nature of special education is constantly evolving and many principals complete their administrative certification program several years before their first appointment (Westberry, 2020).

The remainder of the chapter addresses various ways that principals support special education programming. In addition to reviewing research, the authors invited current and former principals to share details about their work with special education by responding to four questions related to principal roles, principal leadership, principal learning, and principal advice. The survey was administered via an online platform with the option to remain anonymous.

Seven individuals, whose experience spans grade levels and school settings, shared experiences, provided details about things that worked—and didn't—at their schools, and offered recommendations for school principals. Where relevant, their responses are referenced using pseudonyms. The chapter concludes with actionable recommendations and questions to consider.

ROLE OF THE PRINCIPAL

Policy makers and researchers have emphasized improving student achievement and overall school effectiveness as the primary role of the school principal (Dhuey & Smith, 2014; Grissom, Nicholson-Crotty, & Harrington, 2014). Specifically, the role of the principal has been connected to school improvement efforts as well as instructional quality among teachers and staff, which in turn influences student learning and achievement (Grissom & Loeb, 2011).

Principals are responsible for hiring and supervising teachers, evaluating their performance, assigning them to classrooms, and creating teaching schedules, among other tasks (Dhuey & Smith, 2014). Understanding how to differentiate those responsibilities as they apply to teachers in critical need areas, such as special education, is a common barrier, and the lack of related research and guidance makes it an ongoing issue.

Various organizations have published standards and recommendations for principal leadership that address the importance of "all students" (e.g., Council of Chief State School Officers, 2008) or that focus primarily on IEPs and other legal requirements (e.g., National Association of Elementary School Principals; Office of Special Education Programs).

While the research is scant, there are some authors who have published suggestions, such as Sider, Maich, and Morvan's (2017) list of domains related to principals and school-based special education inclusion (i.e., inclusive program delivery, staff collaboration, and parental engagement). Within those domains, the researchers noted several roles for the principal to take on, many of which overlap (e.g., visionary, partner, interpreter, organizer).

The Council for Exceptional Children (2009) established a list of knowledge and skills for special education administrators who have some previous knowledge of special education: leadership and policy, program development and organization, research and inquiry, individual and program evaluation, professional development and ethical practice, and collaboration. Although not specifically written for school administrators, some argue that these standards apply to principal practices due to the responsibility for the education of all students (Glowacki & Hackmann, 2016).

In order to fully support all students, including students with disabilities, school principals must engage in and encourage the practice of collaborating with all stakeholders, including, but not limited to, teachers, instructional assistants and paraprofessionals, administrators, guidance counselors, school psychologists, therapists, and parents. This willingness to collaborate is a key component of various administrative responsibilities related to special education.

Special Education and Principal Responsibilities

School principals are the instructional leaders for all school programs, including special education services. They play a vital role in the advocacy for an inclusive school environment where all students are treated equitably and have access to the resources and instruction they need to be successful. The importance of principals embracing and setting the tone for inclusion is echoed throughout this chapter.

As one survey respondent noted, "You have to have a heart for the true meaning of all means all" (Principal B), while another referenced setting the expectation that "all students are our collective responsibility" (Principal E). The principal makes decisions that directly impact students relating to the allocation of resources, programming, and class placements.

Despite the many ways in which principals are expected to interact with special education programming, most principals enter their positions underprepared to manage or support special education programs. Forced to learn on their own, "or rely on the knowledge and skill of others who may or may not be well informed coaches" (DiPaola, Tschannen-Moran, & Walther-Thomas, 2004, p.7), school leaders can struggle through various incidences involving special education teachers and students.

Although there will be roles and responsibilities that are specific to special education and the principal's knowledge, understanding, and attitude toward the law (i.e., IEP related), there are also "regular principal responsibilities" that can have a direct impact on special education programming and quality, such as teacher evaluation and master scheduling processes.

Evaluation Tools

Teacher effectiveness and evaluation tools are well-researched, generally; however, the research on special education evaluation is minimal, and there is currently no teacher performance measure that has been explicitly developed for use with special education teachers (Semmelroth & Johnson, 2014). Further, there is minimal guidance for school administrators in either state statutes or research about how to facilitate professional growth and support specific to these teachers (Pazey & Cole, 2013).

In the absence of research and standardized measures, some states and organizations have published various documents related to special education teacher evaluation: by establishing professional standards (e.g., Council for Exceptional Children, 2015), by providing recommendations for policy and practice (Westberry, 2020), and by utilizing evaluation processes specifically designed for special education teacher evaluation (Semmelroth & Johnson, 2014).

These documents contained many similarities: including special education teachers in the development of the tool, working collaboratively to agree on performance expectations and criteria, providing support systems, and giving consideration to the unique nature of each special educator's position, setting, caseload, and student population (Snyder & Pufpaff, 2021, Westberry, 2020).

In order to consider the many roles and responsibilities that special education teachers enact, researchers recommend being flexible (Snyder & Pufpaff, 2021). Administrators can demonstrate this flexibility in terms of the instruments (e.g., utilizing supplementary checklists) as well as the data. When evaluating performance related to student growth, for example, the evaluator can look for and incorporate other evidence of teachers' contributions to student learning (e.g., progress monitoring data as related to the IEP).

Next, determine the specifics for your school. What do your special education teachers do each day? Work with them to identify a list. Responses will likely include, in addition to their classes, managing the oversight and progress monitoring of their caseload (including all IEPs and IEP meetings); providing interventions and accommodations; collaborating with parents, general educators, service providers, and the like; and participating in related responsibilities such as evaluations, behavioral assessments, and compliance tasks.

The recommendation to include special education teachers in conversations and decisions regarding the programming at your school repeats throughout this chapter. Both shared decision-making and creating a collaborative culture appear throughout the literature related to transformative leadership, inclusive schools, and the administrator responsibilities that are specific and/or related to special education, such as master scheduling.

Master Schedules

Principals are ultimately responsible for creating the master schedule. The master schedule dictates how the staff, time, and physical spaces are distributed. This allocation is significant as it determines the "fundamental elements of the student experience" such as the teachers and peers they interact, the size of their classes, their access to additional supports, and so on (Pisoni & Conti, 2019, para. 4). However, many principals see scheduling as a logistical exercise rather than an integral component of teaching and learning (Hibbeln, 2020).

Faced with constraints of time and resources, principals often use scheduling as a "sorting mechanism"—classes and teachers remain static despite changing demographics (Hibbeln, 2020, para. 4), which can inadvertently create inequities for students, especially students requiring special education services (Pisoni & Conti, 2019). Several suggestions have been identified as necessary for consideration when principals create schedules based on student needs.

Multiple principals underscored these suggestions in their survey responses: assigning the strongest teachers to work with high-needs students, ensuring that general educators and special educators have time during the workday to plan together, providing common planning opportunities, and asking special education teachers' input.

Developing a student-centered master schedule means scheduling students first and then assigning teachers, balancing class sizes, building class rosters, organizing purposeful class times, and structuring common planning periods for collaboration (Hibbeln, 2020). For students who require extra support, the scheduling team can look for opportunities to embed special education services within the general education classroom (e.g., coteaching, push-in supports) (Brilliante, 2017). Communicate with your special education teachers about what is in place, what they know works, and what they need.

Including special education teachers in important conversations and providing opportunities for them to collaborate with administration and each other are manageable steps that principals can start taking. Research has documented the benefits of collaboration among teachers and principals as it relates to a number of outcomes, including leadership, job satisfaction, and self-efficacy (e.g., Polega et al., 2019; Sider et al., 2017).

Special Education and Self-Efficacy

Bandura (1977) presented the construct of self-efficacy in an effort to explain how people's beliefs about what they are capable of can influence their actions. In the field of education, self-efficacy refers to teachers' beliefs related to their ability to improve children's achievement. Principal self-efficacy, then, describes a set of beliefs that enable a principal to enact policies and procedures that promote the effectiveness of a school.

When it comes to special education and self-efficacy, though, Balt (2000) describes administrators as "wandering around blind, trying to follow the laws but really without a picture . . . like they're putting a jigsaw puzzle together without ever having seen the box top" (p. 72). For the school culture to be genuinely inclusive, principals have to embrace and model practices that have been proven effective for all students, and this begins with building a solid knowledge base grounded in the experience and expertise of others.

Self-efficacy in terms of special education programming is primarily connected to the principal's lack of preparation. Teacher turnover is an ongoing problem in the field of special education, with many former teachers citing lack of support from administration as the reason for leaving (Dahlkamp, Peters, & Schumacher, 2017). This lack of support is often connected to a lack of confidence in administrator leadership and efficacy.

In order to build self-efficacy, principals can start by engaging with the special education experts in the building, both formally and informally. Many of the suggestions included in this chapter serve to increase not only the ability of school leaders to make confident decisions for their special education programs but also the inclusive practices of the larger school community. For example, shared decision-making provides the administrator with an opportunity to learn from those who are experts, and it is also a key component in schools with inclusive communities (Waldron & McLeskey, 2010).

Researchers have noted that the principal's individual self-efficacy has an impact on the school's collective efficacy (Dahlkamp et al., 2017) in the same way the principal's attitude about inclusion impacts the overall inclusivity of the school community (Cobb, 2015; Urton et al., 2014).

Special Education and Inclusion

The word inclusion never appears in IDEA; rather, the document addresses the importance of placing students with disabilities in the LRE. Inclusion is not a legal term; rather, it is both a belief system and a philosophy of service delivery for educating special education students alongside their typically developing peers.

There are varied definitions of inclusion, but the ideas underpinning it include understanding that all students should be welcomed, valued, and included as members of their school communities, participating to the maximum extent possible, with whatever aids may be necessary, supported by a team of professionals invested in making sure that the students succeed (Friend & Pope, 2005).

When the term "inclusion" is used in reference to the LRE, it typically refers to a range of service delivery models that exist along a continuum, ranging from least to most restrictive. IDEA mandates that each student receive services in the LRE, beginning with general education as an option. The increased number of students with disabilities participating in general education classrooms impacts the role of the principal, in that their responsibilities must reflect the same inclusivity.

The 2004 reauthorization of IDEA also included funds to provide academic and behavioral supports to those students who do not receive special education services by way of the RTI model. RTI involves the ongoing monitoring of student progress to determine the effectiveness of an intervention and the need for a change in intervention (or instruction) (Gresham, 2007).

The RTI model established the general education teachers' full responsibility not only for applying a variety of intervention strategies but also for documenting student responsiveness to interventions within each of the three tier levels (McMaster & Wagner, 2007). Horner and Halle (2020) described RTI as the placement of "special education within, rather than appended to, general education" (p. 75).

This shift is largely reflected in the types of responsibilities principals have: ensuring the multitiered system of support (MTSS) has been developed without bias and is grounded in data; working closely with regular and special education teachers, parents, psychologists, and students to effectively manage the process of referrals; and providing support to all involved.

Principals are responsible for monitoring the implementation of students' IEPs and advocating for special education students to have access to general education resources and programs. This may look like embedding supports within general education classrooms. RTI ensures this is happening for all students who need those supports if it is implemented with fidelity.

Tier Two in the multitiered system often involves specialists or interventionists who "push-in" small group instruction to provide necessary specialized instruction for struggling students. A combination of push-in and pull-out (to the resource classroom) is commonly used for supporting special education students, as well.

Taking the push-in model one step further, cotaught classes provide another option for embedding special education in general education settings. Coteaching occurs when the general educator and special educator are both teachers of record, and they jointly deliver instruction to a diverse group of students in a single classroom (Kilanowski-Press, Foote, & Rinaldo, 2010).

Coteaching is a difficult relationship to navigate, however, and prior to scheduling students in these classes, principals must take steps to ensure that their teachers are prepared and confident. Teaching in a cotaught setting requires "a paradigm shift—from teaching in silos to teaching in tandem, from owning the front of the room to sharing space, from sending students with special needs out of the classroom to thoughtfully differentiating for diverse learners" (Murawski & Berhnardt, 2015). Principals can take steps to facilitate this shift through active and visible involvement in planning and implementation.

Regardless of the continuum of settings offered at their schools, principals must identify meaningful opportunities for growth and development. In addition to planning for collaboration time in the master schedule, principals can involve the teachers in conversations about professional development needs and purposes.

The principal is responsible for facilitating a schoolwide inclusive environment to ensure that students with disabilities are fully assimilated within the school community (Bateman & Bateman, 2014). In order to successfully facilitate this inclusivity, school administrators must be willing to develop teachers as leaders within the school and work to develop a collaborative, professional learning community (PLC) to support teacher learning (Waldron & McLeskey, 2010).

Special Education and Collaboration

In the educational context, collaboration refers to teachers working together in groups or teams to improve educational processes and outcomes while learning from each other. Teacher collaboration has been linked to positive outcomes in terms of school culture, student performance, and self-efficacy (Hoppey & McLesky, 2010).

Successful collaboration requires allocated time and specified goals or outcomes. Principals' instructional practices can support collaboration between and among general and special education teachers in many ways (e.g., inclusive community and/or shared vision, common planning, professional development).

Çoban, Özdemir, and Bellibaş (2020) noted that principals' instructional leadership practices enhanced teachers' sense of efficacy both directly and indirectly through teacher collaboration. PLCs are referenced throughout the literature as an effective way to combine collaboration with professional development (Hallam et al., 2015).

Etienne Wenger coined the term PLC to represent "in a nutshell: . . . groups of people who share a concern or a passion for something they do and learn how to do it better as they interact regularly" (Wenger & Wenger, 2015, p. 1). These school-based teams are designed to support students using evidence-based problem-solving strategies (DuFour & Marzano, 2009). PLCs vary in format. For example, PLCs might focus on instruction, IEP teams, students with academic or behavioral difficulties, or data teams that support teaching and learning.

These collaborative efforts provide opportunities for the various stakeholders, using problem-solving strategies, to make instructional decisions about learning outcomes (DuFour & Marzano, 2009). As teachers share their experiences while learning with and from their colleagues, they simultaneously strengthen their self-efficacy related to the topic. Several studies, such as Voelkel Jr. and Chrispeels (2017), indicate that these communities also predict greater collective efficacy.

Principals have an opportunity, and a responsibility, to facilitate discussions related to students with disabilities in the context of PLCs (DuFour & Marzano, 2009). In order to establish an inclusive school community, school administrators must model their belief that inclusion involves all teachers and all students in both planning and practice.

Principals should participate in school-based PLCs to ensure that they remain connected with the collaboration among teachers. PLCs also provide a format for the principals to expand their knowledge of special education laws, regulations, and related pedagogy. In addition, principals can benefit from participating in PLCs comprising other principals who share common goals and needs. Inclusion requires leadership from states, districts, and school leaders, so principals should use all resources, including collaboration with their colleagues, to find appropriate training or activities to address their needs (Bublitz, 2016).

In the survey, several principals identified collaboration in the context of common planning as an integral part of their work with special education programming, noting that it "creates trust between teachers and administration and results that are student-centered" (Principal C). Research emphasizes the importance of trust as it relates to teacher collaboration and principal support as well (e.g., Çoban et al., 2020). Inclusive schools are most effective when school principals build supportive and collaborative relationships with all members of the school community.

Special Education and Relationships

Samuels (2018) suggests that while knowledge of special education law and best practices are necessary for principals, the single most effective strategy for supporting special education is to establish relationships with families. Developing a trusting relationship is an important step that encourages families to be more flexible and willing to take risks relating to new strategies that might help their child. Open communication is important in developing positive and authentic relationships, especially given the overwhelming nature of the IEP process for many parents and families.

Principals can build trusting relationships through their ongoing interactions with parents. Parents want a welcoming principal who knows and cares about their child. Principals who are visible and engaged with students and parents on a daily basis are more likely to develop positive relationships. For instance, principals who have a daily ritual of greeting students and parents are perceived to be more authentically connected to the needs of students (Rodriquez, Murakami-Ramalho, & Ruff, 2009).

Some parents feel intimidated by the formal nature of IEP meetings and have limited knowledge of special education processes. Open communication is important in developing positive and authentic relationships with the parents and families. Once these positive relationships have been established with parents, it is easier to navigate the often-complicated conversations that need to occur during IEP meetings.

Principals should foster open communication with parents to ensure their role as equal team members of the IEP. Establishing open communication in advance to formal meetings demonstrates respect for the parents and an appreciation of their input into the needs and abilities of their child. Open communication also demonstrates that educators authentically care about students, something validated by Principal D's assertion that parents want to feel validated, supported, and heard. Diliberto and Brewer (2012) identify several strategies for building rapport with parents, namely:

> Contacting parents prior to the beginning of the school year, emphasizing an open-door policy, encouraging parental visits and participation during lunch, classroom activities, and field trips, and providing several forms of contact information (e.g., email, telephone numbers with available times). (pp. 129–30)

LEADERSHIP

The topics discussed in this chapter and the corresponding recommendations align with characteristics and practices identified as key components for inclusive educational leadership. Special education teachers often report the main reasons they leave the field are dissatisfaction with their administrators, feeling overwhelmed and marginalized, and having a lack of appropriate resources (Cornelius & Gustafson, 2021). Relatedly, general education teachers tend to develop negative attitudes about inclusion due to their perception of not being supported or trained appropriately (deBoer, Pijl, & Minnaert, 2011).

Research related to educational leadership posits that school principals should be strong instructional leaders who have the capacity and expertise to provide support and professional development for teachers (Council of Chief State School Officers, 2008). Ajuwon and Oyinlade (2016) identified "good listening skills, good presentation skills, and [a] participative decision-making style" (p. 3) as leadership skills and behaviors all principals need.

Teachers need ongoing administrative support to be successful, and, as students with disabilities are the responsibility of all educators in the building, principals can play a part in ensuring that both special and general education teachers feel supported. Principal support has been identified as the key for assuring that teachers are appropriately differentiating instruction and addressing problematic behaviors in students with disabilities (DiPaola et al., 2004).

RECOMMENDATIONS FOR GROWTH

Although the suggestions detailed below are separated into categories, overlap related to the overarching goal of creating and leading inclusive school communities occurs, especially in regard to special education programming. In that sense, the first recommendation for growth in this area has to do with establishing a schoolwide community of inclusivity.

Promote an Inclusive School Community

Exceptional students should and need to feel that they are not only a part of the school but that they are valued and loved.

—Principal B

Research has demonstrated not only the impact an inclusive environment can have on student and faculty experiences but also that the principal's attitude about inclusion can have marked effects on the way inclusion is or is not implemented (Cobb, 2015). Given that each school setting is different, principals should identify strategies specific to their student and teacher population for increasing access and providing options.

The process of developing an inclusive school community begins with recognizing and accepting differences, ensuring equitable conditions for all those in the community, and actively embracing the ideas that underscore inclusion. To promote an inclusive school community, principals must be active models of inclusivity, which includes ensuring that teachers receive the appropriate resources and training to successfully support inclusion in their classrooms.

Facilitate Family Engagement

As principal, you want to engage with students and families regularly to get their feedback about what's working.

—Principal E

It is imperative for school principals to recognize that a truly inclusive school community cannot exist without the support and engagement of all the people who are involved with the community, namely family members or other individuals responsible for securing a student's education. Allowing for authentic engagement with family members underscores the importance of inclusivity as a school value and provides a framework for putting inclusion into practice.

Principals can utilize a number of informal strategies to determine how best to partner with the larger school community (e.g., town hall meetings, focus groups, and invited participation at events), as well as more formal means of doing so, such as developing or adapting a tool to determine the needs that are specific to the school and its community.

Develop a School-Specific Needs Assessment

Always make decisions for what is in the best interest of children.

—Principal D

In order to effectively support all students, including those with disabilities, principals should develop a needs assessment specific to their schools. Various resources are available for developing needs assessments, including the Office of Elementary and Secondary Education (U.S. Department of Education, 2020).

Generally speaking, the assessment should identify academic and behavioral needs, evaluate available resources (human and material), develop a plan for the professional development of teachers and administrators, and establish how to measure progress and success. The results of this assessment can then provide guidance for establishing inclusive processes for administrative responsibilities such as master scheduling.

Schedule with Student-Centered Approach

I rely heavily on the expertise of my special education teachers when making decisions that affect our students with special needs.

—*Principal C*

Creating a master schedule is often considered a primarily logistical task; however, in order to establish more inclusive practices at the schoolwide level, principals should be more deliberate about scheduling in terms of the school's diversity (ability, cultural background, language, etc.).

To do this, principals should begin by scheduling students first, according to the needs of the students and the principles of inclusion. Only then should the principal assign teachers, doing it in such a way that classes are balanced according to size, diversity, and teacher knowledge, skills, and dispositions. Further, the master schedule should incorporate details that support the general and special education teachers in the building.

For instance, the principal should consider ways to include unencumbered time in the schedule that allows special education teachers to plan and collaborate with their general education counterparts. Principals of larger schools with multiple special education teachers should examine various ways of dividing the case load of students requiring special education. Taking into account the teaching strengths of teachers or the number of students in need of services in different classes or subjects can determine the best division of the case load.

Provide Opportunities for Collaboration

At our school collaboration and planning are a part of our culture.

—*Principal B*

Even if school principals take various steps to ensure the school community is inclusive and supportive of all students, they must also be purposeful about ensuring that teachers feel supported and prepared for a diverse student population. This process can be done in multiple ways, beginning with the scheduling of common planning time between general and special education teachers who work with the same students.

In terms of teacher preparation and the knowledge and skills necessary for providing appropriate instruction to students with disabilities, principals can use the information from the needs assessment and interactions with their teachers to identify effective systems of support (e.g., PLCs). Similarly, principals can plan professional development activities that meet the specific needs of their teachers and school community. Principals can benefit from actively participating in these professional development activities alongside teachers, as well.

Maintain Teacher Quality

> *The most important role of the principal is hiring the highest quality teachers and setting the expectation that all students are our collective responsibility.*
>
> —Principal E

To truly establish a schoolwide inclusive community, school principals must recognize the importance of recruiting and retaining quality special education teachers. Despite the critical shortage in special education teachers, or perhaps because of it, principals should apply the same student-centered focus for hiring the individuals who will fill special education positions, which will establish a more solid base in terms of both teacher quality and student achievement.

Equally important are the people who fill instructional assistant positions in special education classrooms. Principals should work with the special education department to identify criteria and include them in the hiring process. Teacher assistants spend just as much time in the classroom and with students, so including your teachers in hiring decisions makes it clear that their opinions are valued and that you trust their experience.

Ensuring that positions are filled by quality special educators is not the same as ensuring those teachers stay at your school, however. The field of special education has a high turnover rate, and many teachers who leave the field cite the lack of support from and belief in administration as a reason behind their decision. Therefore, it is important that principals determine how to best support their special education program. Building an inclusive community requires that principals engage with and learn from their special education teachers to determine their support needs.

Continue to Learn and Grow

I had no idea how much special education teachers did in a day until I spent time with them.

—*Principal C*

Perhaps the most important recommendation for school principals is to actively seek out ways to improve their understanding of the diverse needs of today's student population, especially as it relates to special education programming. While there are certainly formal means of doing this (e.g., professional development and online learning), principals should also utilize the informal resources available to them within their own school communities.

For instance, principals can engage in conversations with their special education faculty and staff to learn more about the specifics of their school's program and updates related to legal requirements. To more adequately prepare for the evaluation of special education classrooms, principals should spend time visiting, observing, and interacting in those classrooms so that they have a better sense of what is "normal" and expected, as well as what is unexpected, and how teachers respond in those situations.

A strategy that can help novice principals, or those with limited background in special education, is teaming with an experienced special education teacher, a veteran principal, or a district special education consultant to learn how to conduct effective classroom observations. Another important source of support for school administrators are other principals who share similar challenges and most likely can benefit from engaging in the same professional development. PLCs comprising groups of principals provide opportunities to learn together about relevant topics including those related to special education.

Principal support of special education and an inclusive school culture is dependent on ongoing professional growth relating to special education legislation and practices. Furthermore, the principal's oversight is necessary to ensure that special education services are appropriately implemented by all staff members. Professional development provides a means for supporting staff members in their delivery of specialized instruction and related services (Bateman & Bateman, 2014).

CONCLUSION

Principals are ultimately responsible for the success of their schools and all students in the building. These myriad responsibilities include special education programming and oversight, which many principals are underprepared for implementing. Federal legislation and individual state requirements have prompted exponential growth in the inclusion of students with special needs in the general education classroom; however, school principals continue to express discomfort or a lack of preparation regarding their roles related to special education.

Previous research regarding this growth in the inclusion of students with disabilities in general education classrooms highlighted three ways to enable better preparation and self-efficacy: **Show Me** what it is that I am supposed to be doing; **Give Me** the tools to do these things; and **Let Me** practice doing them on my own (Stefanski, 2014). Principals need the same time and opportunity to learn about special education needs in their buildings as teachers need the same to become proficient in differentiation.

This chapter has been arranged as a resource for school principals using the same framework, with sections written and organized to show potential issues and underscore related responsibilities as documented by research, guidance documents, and voluntary survey responses (Show Me), and to provide guidance in terms of suggestions and recommendations (Give Me). Finally, readers are invited to consider the topics covered herein (i.e., principal responsibilities, self-efficacy, beliefs about inclusion, collaboration, relationships, instructional leadership) in the discussion questions following this section (Let Me).

REFLECTION QUESTIONS

1. What strategies would promote inclusion in your school? What are the unique assets and characteristics of your students, staff, and community?
2. How could you facilitate family engagement? What are the strengths and challenges your school community presents related to family engagement?
3. What special education needs do your school data reveal? What goals would help you address these needs? How will you assess progress toward meeting these goals?
4. What steps could you implement to develop a student-centered master schedule?
5. How can you provide opportunities for ongoing collaboration between special education and general education teachers?
6. What steps will you take in the next school year to develop your knowledge of special education policies and practices?

REFERENCES

Ajuwon, P. M., & Oyinlade, A. O. (2016). Cross-cultural comparison of effective leadership in schools for children with blindness or low vision in the United States and Nigeria. *International Journal of Special Education, 31*(3), 1–26.

Balt, S. D. (2000). *Preparing principals for leadership in special education* (Doctoral dissertation, University of California).

Bandura, A. (1977). Self-efficacy: Toward a unifying theory of behavioral change. *Psychological review, 84*(2), 191.

Bateman, D. F., & Bateman, C. F. (2014). *A principal's guide to special education.* Third Edition. Virginia: Council for Exceptional Children.

Brendle, J. (2015). A survey of response to intervention team members' effective practices in rural elementary schools. *Rural Special Education Quarterly, 34*(2), 3–8.

Brilliante, P. (2017). *The essentials: Supporting young children with disabilities in the classroom.* National Association for the Education of Young Children.

Brunner, R., & Bateman, D. (2020). Principals must build a range of knowledge to navigate and deliver special education appropriately. *Principal, 99*(3). www.naesp.org

Bublitz, G. (2016). *Effective strategies for district leadership to create successful inclusion models: Special education directors and school reform in context of least restrictive environment* (Doctoral dissertation, Loyola University Chicago).

Çoban, Ö., Özdemir, N., & Bellibaş, M. Ş. (2020). Trust in principals, leaders' focus on instruction, teacher collaboration, and teacher self-efficacy: Testing a multilevel mediation model. *Educational Management Administration & Leadership*, 1–21.

Cobb, C. (2015). Principals play many parts: a review of the research on school principals as special education leaders 2001–2011. *International Journal of Inclusive Education, 19*(3), 213–34.

Cornelius, K. E., & Gustafson, J. A. (2021). Relationships with school administrators: Leveraging knowledge and data to self-advocate. *Teaching Exceptional Children, 53*(3), 206–14.

Council of Chief State School Officers [CCSSO] (2008). *Performance expectations and indicators for education leaders.* Washington, DC: Council of Chief State School Officers.

Dahlkamp, S., Peters, M., & Schumacher, G. (2017). Principal self-efficacy, school climate, and teacher retention: A multi-level analysis. *Alberta Journal of Educational Research, 63*(4), 357–76.

deBoer, A., Pijl, S. J., & Minnaert, A. (2011). Regular primary teachers' attitudes towards inclusive education: A review of literature. *International Journal of Inclusive Education, 15*(3), 331–53.

DeMatthews, D. E., Kotok, S., & Serafini, A. (2020). Leadership preparation for special education and inclusive schools: Beliefs and recommendations from successful principals. *Journal of Research on Leadership Education, 15*(4), 303–29.

Dhuey, E., & Smith, J. (2014). How important are school principals in the production of student achievement? *Canadian Journal of Economics, 47*(2), 634–63.

Diliberto, J. A., & Brewer, D. (2012). Six tips for successful IEP meetings. *Teaching Exceptional Children, 44*(4), 30–37.

DiPaola, M., Tschannen-Moran, M., & Walther-Thomas, C. (2004). School principals and special education: Creating the context for academic success. *Focus on Exceptional Children, 37*(1), 1–10.

DuFour, R., & Marzano, R. J. (2009). High-leverage strategies for principal leadership. *Educational Leadership, 66*(5), 62–68.

Friend, M., & Pope, K. L. (2005). Creating schools in which all students can succeed. *Kappa Delta Pi Record, 41*(2), 56–61.

Glowacki, H., & Hackmann, D. G. (2016). The effectiveness of special education teacher evaluation processes: Perspectives from elementary principals. *Planning & Changing, 47*(3/4), 191–209.

Gresham, F. M. (2007). Evolution of the response-to-intervention concept: Empirical foundations and recent developments. In S. Jimerson, M. Burns, & A. VanDerHeyden (Eds.), *Handbook of response to intervention: The science and practice of assessment and intervention*, pp. 10–24. New York: Springer.

Grissom, J. A., & Loeb, S. (2011). Triangulating principal effectiveness: How perspectives of parents, teachers, and assistant principals identify the central importance of managerial skills. *American Educational Research Journal, 48*(5), 1091-1123.

Grissom, J. A., Nicholson-Crotty, S., & Harrington, J. R. (2014). Estimating the effects of No Child Left Behind on teachers' work environments and job attitudes. *Educational Evaluation and Policy Analysis, 36*(4), 417–36.

Hallam, P. R., Smith, H. R., Hite, J. M., Hite, S. J., & Wilcox, B. R. (2015). Trust and collaboration in PLC teams: Teacher relationships, principal support, and collaborative benefits. *NASSP bulletin, 99*(3), 193–216.

Hibbeln, C. (2020). Mastering the master schedule: Improving instruction and strengthening culture through the master schedule. *Educational Leadership, 77*(9), 36–40.

Hoppey, D., & McLeskey, J. (2010). A case study of principal leadership in an effective inclusive school. *The Journal of Special Education, 46*(4), 245–56.

Horner, R. H., & Halle, J. W. (2020). Implications of emerging educational reforms for individuals with severe disabilities. *Research & Practice for Persons with Severe Disabilities, 45*(2), 75–80.

Individuals with Disabilities Education Act of 2004 [IDEA] (2004). Retrieved from http://idea.ed.gov/

Johnson, E., & Semmelroth, C. L. (2014). Special education teacher evaluation: Why it matters, what makes it challenging, and how to address these challenges. *Assessment for effective intervention, 39*(2), 71–82.

Kilanowski-Press, L., Foote, C. J., & Rinaldo, V. J. (2010). Inclusion classrooms and teachers: A survey of current practices. *International Journal of Special Education, 25*(3), 43–56.

McMaster, K. & Wagner, D. (2007). Monitoring response to general education instruction. In S. Jimerson, M. Burns, & A. Van Der Hayden (Eds.), *Handbook of response to intervention: The science and practice of assessment and intervention.* New York: Springer Science and Business Media, LLC.

Murawski, W. W., & Bernhardt, P. (2015). An administrator's guide to co-teaching. *Educational Leadership, 73*(4), 30–34.

Murphy, C. R. (2018). Transforming inclusive education: Nine tips to enhance school leaders' ability to effectively lead inclusive special education programs. *Journal of Educational Research and Practice, 8*(1), 87–100.

Pazey, B. L., & Cole, H. A. (2013). The role of special education training in the development of socially just leaders: Building an equity consciousness in educational leadership programs. *Educational Administration Quarterly, 49*(2), 243–71.

Pisoni, A., & Conti, D. (2019, April 20). *What does your school schedule say about equity? More than you think.* EdSurge. Retrieved from https://www.edsurge.com/news/2019-04-20-what-does-your-school-schedule-say-about-equity-more-than-you-think

Polega, M., Neto, R. D. C. A., Brilowski, R., & Baker, K. (2019). Principals and teamwork among teachers: An exploratory study. *Revista@ mbienteeducação, 12*(2), 12–32.

Rodriquez, M. A., Murakami-Ramalho, E., & Ruff, W. G. (2009). Leading with heart: Urban elementary principals as advocates for students. *Educational Considerations, 36*(2), 8–13.

Samuels, C. A. (2018). The important role principals play in special education. *Education Week, 38*(9), 26–28.

Sider, S., Maich, K., & Morvan, J. (2017). School principals and students with special education needs: Leading inclusive schools. *Canadian Journal of Education/Revue canadienne de l'éducation, 40*(2), 1–31.

Snyder, R. A., & Pufpaff, L. A. (2021). Current State of High Stakes Teacher Evaluation for Special Education Teachers. *The Journal of Special Education Apprenticeship, 10*(1), 2.

Stefanski, A. (2014). *Inclusion as a reform: How secondary general educators make sense of and enact their roles as teachers of students with disabilities* (Doctoral dissertation, University of Maryland, College Park).

Sumbera, M. J., Pazey, B. L., & Lashley, C. (2014). How building principals made sense of free and appropriate public education in the least restrictive environment. *Leadership and Policy in Schools, 13*(3), 297–333.

Urton, K., Wilbert, J., & Hennemann, T. (2014). Attitudes towards inclusion and self-efficacy of principals and teachers. *Learning Disabilities: A Contemporary Journal, 12*(2), 151–168.

U.S. Department of Education (n.d.). *History: Twenty-five years of progress in educating children with disabilities through IDEA.* Retrieved from http://www2.ed.gov/policy/speced/leg/idea/history.pdf

U.S. Department of Education (2020). *School improvement: Needs assessment.* Retrieved from https://oese.ed.gov/resources/oese-technical-assistance-centers/state-support-network/resources/school-improvement-needs-assessment/

Voelkel Jr., R. H., & Chrispeels, J. H. (2017). Understanding the link between professional learning communities and teacher collective efficacy. *School Effectiveness and School Improvement, 28*(4), 505–26.

Waldron, N. L., & McLeskey, J. (2010). Establishing a collaborative school culture through comprehensive school reform. *Journal of Educational and Psychological Consultation, 20*(1), 58–74.

Wenger, E., & Wenger, B. (2015). Communities of Practice: A Brief Introduction. Web. Retrieved from http://wenger-trayner.com/wp-content/uploads/2015/04/07-Brief-introduction-to- communities-of-practice.pdf

Westberry, L. A. (2020). *Putting the pieces together: A systems approach to school leadership*. Rowman & Littlefield.

Williams, J. M. (2015). *Attitude and perceptions of public school principals in Illinois toward inclusion of students with disabilities in the general education classroom* (Doctoral dissertation, McKendree University).

Chapter Seven

Instructional Supervision

Supporting a Culture of Teaching and Learning

Christine LeBlanc and Brennan Davis, Columbia College

INTRODUCTION

Leadership and learning are indispensable to each other.

—John F. Kennedy

The primary responsibility of a school principal is to facilitate school improvement through the support of teaching and learning (DuFour & Marzano, 2009; Gordon & Espinoza, 2020; Zepeda, 2016). Instructional supervision and building teacher capacity are integral factors in improving student achievement.

The school influences that contribute the most to improved student learning are classroom instruction and leadership (Honig & Rainey, 2020; Leithwood & Strauss, 2009). "Effective principals support teaching and learning" with the continuous support and development of teachers (Zepeda, 2016, p. 26). Principals must go beyond the traditional role of school manager and focus on the continued support and development of teachers (Westberry, 2020; Zepeda, 2016). Therefore, the role of the principal as an instructional leader is integral for school improvement:

> Instructional supervision . . . ensures that high expectations for instruction are being met and a platform for providing continuous feedback to help teachers continue to grow in their teaching practices. Students benefit because they are served in an academic setting where they receive a high level of instruction and both teaching and student learning data are monitored frequently. (J. White, personal communication, November 2021)

Characteristics of Effective Supervision

Collegial supervision is characterized by collaborative relationships between teachers and administrators and is linked to more successful schools, according to Glickman, Gordon, and Ross-Gordon (2018). This collaborative supervision supports a schoolwide focus on instructional improvement where teachers are active learners who reflect and improve their teaching practices in a proactive manner (Marzano, 2011; Ozdemir & Shain, 2020; Zepeda, 2016).

In an ongoing survey study of principals in South Carolina, the authors gathered data regarding the challenges, opportunities, and insights principals hold after several years in their positions. The findings of this study, based on the responses of the initial eight participants, are shared throughout this chapter as personal communications. The eight principals serve in a high school (one) and elementary schools (seven) located in central South Carolina. Their schools represent a diverse range of demographics and programing including three Title I schools, three art integration schools, a science, technology, engineering, and mathematics (STEM) school, and one Montessori school.

When asked to identify the characteristics of an effective instructional leader, these principals shared that instructional supervision strategies play a key role. They believe that principals should be knowledgeable of curriculum and have a "plethora of research-based instructional strategies in his or her toolbox and can coach teachers to utilize these strategies effectively."

The participants of the study survey also suggested that principals hold high expectations on teachers to implement effective instructional strategies, monitor student progress, and provide differentiated instruction to meet the individual learning needs of students. These principals also noted the importance of providing personalized support to teachers through professional development (PD) and ongoing feedback related to their instructional practices.

The Principal's Role in Effective Instructional Supervision

DuFour and Marzano (2009) suggest that principals engage in a continuous process to refine their supervisory skills through teacher development. Principals impact the quality of teaching and improve student performance through their supervisory actions that include PD, collaboration, and evaluation of teaching and learning (Ozdemir & Sahin, 2020).

Instructional leaders develop authentic relationships with teachers based on respect and compassion with the common goal of improved student learning (St. Clair, 2020). Furthermore, principals establish effective supervisory skills through their "knowledge of best practices, compassion for teacher workload, understanding of the many demands teachers feel, responsive[ness] to data which drives instruction, and holding staff accountable for quality teaching and learning" (P. Roberts, personal communication, 2021).

As principals create a schoolwide culture of learning, it is possible to differentiate the support teachers receive based on individual needs of both the teachers and students (Ozdemir & Sahin, 2020). Just as teachers are expected to personalize teaching to meet the needs of students, it is important for principals to personalize teacher support.

Principals' individualized support of teachers develops from data they collect from classroom observations, walkthroughs, collaborative planning, lesson plan review, and mentoring teachers. These data help the principal to determine how to differentiate PD for all teachers, including those who are new to the profession and veteran teachers.

EFFECTIVE INSTRUCTIONAL SUPERVISORY PRACTICES

Instructional improvement is dependent on how the principal implements supervisory practices. DuFour and Marzano (2009) maintain that strategically providing PD opportunities and monitoring progress through principal support correlates to the effective supervision of schools. Remember, this support should be personalized.

Professional Development

The PD experiences, when aligned to the specific needs of both the students and the teachers, cultivate an environment conducive to improved teaching and learning. PD that encourages the transfer of teacher learning to their practice includes a focus on subject content, strategies to teach content, hands-on, active learning, ongoing PD over the course of a semester or year, and collaborative opportunities for teachers to learn together in professional learning communities (PLCs) (Baker & Bloom, 2017).

These PD experiences are most effective when implemented in a continuous cycle. This begins with analyzing teacher and student data and setting goals aligned to these data. Principals can support this process prior to the collection of data through their efforts to establish trusting and reflective relationships with teachers. Teachers will be more receptive to PD when they have input into its content and when they feel it will help their instructional practice.

The cycle continues with individual and collaborative learning related to the goals followed by opportunities to implement new strategies in classrooms. Then principals and teachers analyze the effectiveness of the new strategies and make adjustments as needed to instructional practice (Hirsh

& Crow, 2017). This continuous cycle of PD must accommodate for both new and experienced teachers. Teachers are more likely to buy into PD that is relative and personalized (Westberry, 2020). Principals' consistent and intentional implementation of these processes correlates to improved teacher performance (Glickman et al., 2018; Zepeda, 2016).

When principals provide these embedded PD opportunities as part of the typical school day, there is an increase in collaboration, reflective practice, and individualized learning among teachers (Westberry, 2020; Zepeda, 2016). The effectiveness of these PD opportunities depends on the teachers' comfort with taking risks to try new strategies. Therefore, the way principals build trust with teachers and facilitate collaboration is important.

Principals begin this process with the development of a strategic PD plan that meets these specific needs of the students and teachers while promoting collaboration and reflection between teachers and administrators.

Strategic Planning

Strategic planning helps the principal set appropriate and realistic goals for improving teachers' instructional practices. Miles and Frank (2008) suggest five components to guide strategic plans toward improving the quality of instruction:

> Determine your school's highest-priority academic needs; assess how well your resources are aligned with your academic needs; set concrete goals that meet your highest-priority needs; identify and evaluate actions for accomplishing your goals; and create a strategy by choosing a set of actions that works for you. (pp. 156–57)

The highest-priority academic needs are determined through an analysis of student performance data, which takes a comprehensive look at data across grade levels and demographic groups to identify areas of strengths and challenges. In addition, principals should consider teacher data points to determine their individualized PD needs (Westberry, 2020).

Setting goals to improve instruction depends on the specific needs and priorities of the teachers and students. A school with high student performance and strong teacher capacity is ready to focus on teacher collaboration and strengthen the leadership skills of teachers. On the other hand, a school with low student performance and low teacher capacity will need to focus on the PD of teachers to strengthen the teaching skills (Miles & Frank, 2008). Most schools have both low- and high-performing students and teachers; therefore, principals must use a differentiated approach of matching support as appropriate.

PLCs to Build Teacher Capacity

PLCs create opportunities for PD and collaborative discussions around student data. PLC meetings provide an authentic process for teachers and administrators to analyze what students know and need (Grissom, Egalite, & Lindsay, 2021). Glickman et al. (2018) identified six characteristics of PLCs: shared beliefs, values, and norms; distributed, supportive leadership; collective learning; collaboration related to teaching strategies focused on student learning and collaboration.

Principals utilize PLC meetings to strengthen teamwork between teachers, creating a synergetic process that leads to innovation. Kempen and Steyn (2017) found that collaborative work in schools changes the thinking of individuals "working together, expertise and resources are exchanged resulting in enhanced levels of thinking and . . . creative solutions" (p.168). Solvason and Kingston (2020) found evidence that collaborations "can enable intellectual as well as emotional development and resilience in the professionals involved" (p. 104).

Trusting relationships and open communication are essential for effective collaboration to occur in PLCs (Solvason & Kingston, 2020). Principals can use PLCs to "build trust, empower teachers, and encourage reflection" (Ozdemir & Sahin, 2020, p. 19). Additionally, these meetings can connect learning opportunities and differentiated support to strengthen teachers' knowledge of content and instruction.

The structure of teams varies according to the school size and level. Teachers at the same grade level or content areas share common instructional goals and resources, so it behooves them to collaborate. Principals foster collaboration by using various configurations of PLC teams such as grade-level planning, vertical grade-level data meetings, school leadership data meetings, and even PLCs involving all staff. PLCs provide a forum for teachers to share ideas or ask for assistance.

Secondary collaborative teams are traditionally structured according to subject areas. One South Carolina principal from the author's ongoing survey study shared as follows: "We set the expectation that teachers will collaborate weekly with their team. We also provide time for vertical alignment (of learning standards) across grade levels" (B. Parks, personal communication, 2021). However, structuring collaborative teams based on shared students allows teams to focus more on individual student progress (Miles & Frank, 2008).

Lesson Planning

Much of the collaboration that takes place in schools revolves around teachers planning instruction. Principals play an important role in supporting instruction through their expectations and support of the lesson planning process by providing time, resources, and expert support. Principals foster growth in lesson planning by encouraging protocols such as the backward design model developed by Wiggins and McTighe (2005). A South Carolina principal from the survey study believes that lesson planning should be collaborative:

> Collaborative planning allows teams of teachers to examine student data, identify learning goals and objectives, develop common assessments, and identify instructional strategies. We provide protective times to collaborate and the resources they need to make this time successful. (P. Roberts, personal communication, 2021)

Principals communicate the expectations relating to the acceptable structure of lesson plans, requirements for turning lesson plans in for review by the school leadership team, and the feedback provided to teachers (Miles & Frank, 2008). "Each team member brings ideas to the table and the grade level is on the same page with content but may have their own twist of presentation" (P. Roberts, personal communication, November 2021).

Principals in high-performing schools find ways to increase the amount of time scheduled for teachers to collaborate. "A first step in supporting collaborative planning is structuring common and uninterrupted planning times so teachers can collaborate to develop effective instruction" (C. Woods, Elementary Principal, personal communication, 2021). Principals can increase the amount of planning time by double-blocking planning periods or combining planning periods with noninstructional times. Some districts build early release or late start schedules into the school calendar to accomplish this (Miles & Frank, 2008).

Collaborative lesson planning is of particular importance for new or inexperienced teachers who are often overwhelmed and lack the resources or experience to develop rigorous and appropriate lessons (Goodwin, 2012). "Common planning time is a start. It is essential with administration and the instructional support team modeling what is expected of the teachers in their teams or school" (M. Keith, personal communication, 2021).

Developing Teacher Leaders

Providing support for all teachers can be an overwhelming challenge for a principal who must manage multiple responsibilities at the same time. Principals can effectively supervise a school's instructional practices by using a distributive leadership style to develop effective teams of teachers (DuFour & Marzano, 2009). Creating collaborative teacher teams is a means for increasing teachers' instructional capacity while delegating critical responsibilities.

Teacher leadership also serves an important role in school improvement; principals should motivate teachers to examine problems with a different lens. Leadership helps to find ways to work smarter, not harder. Principals can encourage teacher leadership through team, committee or task force leadership, school improvement council membership, and mentorship.

Developing teacher leaders begins with the principal "defining teacher teams and assigning responsibilities and developing yearlong schedules for common and PD time (Miles & Frank, 2008, p. 165). Danielson (2007) defined teacher leadership as a "set of skills demonstrated by teachers who continue to teach students but also have an influence that extends beyond their own classrooms within their own school and elsewhere" (p. 12).

S. Fields uses a gradual release of responsibility with her teachers because "team leaders are more than information distributors. They help make school decisions and facilitate data conversations" (personal communication, November 2021). Principals develop teacher leaders by modeling and coaching effective supervisory behavior (Honig & Rainey, 2020). This modeling and coaching should take place in collaborative decision-making processes.

When principals encourage teachers to develop leadership skills, "they become empowered to lead change, improving themselves and their students' development" (Halpern, Szecsi, and Mak, 2021, p. 670). Teacher leaders who feel motivated by their own growth tend to encourage other teachers on their teams to implement new strategies (Gewertz, 2021; Solvason & Kingston, 2020).

> The best way that I've found to grow teacher leaders is to delegate tasks, provide support and feedback. After assigning tasks and setting expectations for outcomes, it is important to allow the teacher to have some freedom to make decisions, involve other stakeholders, and implement the plan. Oftentimes, teachers are afraid to fail and I encourage them by sharing that we all make mistakes . . . it is important to maximize the teacher leader" potential by utilizing the leadership strengths and weaknesses strategically. Reflecting on the leadership experiences is critical for helping grow teacher leaders! (J. White, personal communication, November 2021)

Learning Conversations to Promote Reflection

Principals use learning conversations as a supervisory practice to grow teachers' reflective practices. Learning conversations can occur organically throughout the school day as the principal encounters teachers, and they can also occur strategically in planned times. The principal coaches and encourages teachers' reflection and goal-setting during these conversations (Costa et al., 2015). Principals facilitate the conversations by asking open-ended questions and paraphrasing the teachers' responses. The conversation should be respectful and safe to encourage honest and open communication.

The interpersonal behaviors that principals use in these learning conversations, including "listening, clarifying, encouraging, reflecting, presenting, problem solving, negotiating, directing, standardizing, and reinforcing" strengthens reflection (Glickman et al., 2018, pp. 114–15). Principals can strategically use communication skills such as paraphrasing, open-ended questioning, and mirroring nonverbal body language to encourage reflection.

Principals should use appropriate behaviors for individual characteristics of teacher(s) and situations. Principals can intentionally use learning conversations during PLCs, faculty meetings, or informal interactions between the principal and the teachers. Teachers who engage in reflective conversations with their principals are more likely to transfer these reflective practices into their classroom and ask more thought-provoking questions to their students (Costa et al., 2015).

For instance, P. Roberts, as study participant, uses interactive strategies such as "three plusses and a wish" during meetings to help teachers focus on positive attributes of their teaching and to consider areas of growth, while C. Fields has teachers video tape themselves and provide reflection (personal communication, November 2021).

Another principal from the survey study, L. Derrick, asks her teachers reflective questions, such as "How do you ensure that all of your students are engaged in the learning . . . etc.? How might you revise this lesson to . . .? Tell me more about. . . . What is a strength from the lesson you taught?" (personal communication, November 2021). Reflection can be facilitated in a variety of ways:

> With each observation, I have teachers reflect on the overall lesson. . . . I then ask teachers to share their student data from quick check formative assessments to facilitate reflection based on data of how students did. The data encourages authentic reflection and is live information to show how successful the lesson was. As teachers reflect, it opens the door for conversation regarding what more effective strategies could have been used or next steps for improving the teacher's instructional practices. (J. White, personal communication, 2021)

Instructional Rounds

Instructional rounds occur when principals' classroom observations encourage collaboration and strengthen instructional practice, which allows teachers to compare and reflect on "their own instructional practices with those of the teachers they observe" (Marzano, 2011, p. 80). Instructional rounds can be facilitated by the principal, an instructional coach, or a lead teacher whom the teachers respect and trust. The observed teacher is someone who has volunteered and is considered a "master" teacher. The instructional round works best with a small group of three to five teachers.

The group observes instruction for ten to fifteen minutes, with each observer taking observation notes. After the observation, the group exits the classroom and the leader facilitates a reflective debriefing, taking care not to evaluate the observed teacher. Marzano (2011) suggests that the debriefing focuses on a "pluses and delta" format where the teachers share positive things they observed and questions or concerns they have regarding the use of a strategy (p. 81). The round ends with the teachers identifying instructional strategies they will either continue to use or new strategies they will implement in their own classroom. According to principal P. Roberts, "The most powerful tool we have used is teacher's instructional rounds. We observe other teachers in the school once a month in a non-threatening, professional growth model" (personal communication, November 2021).

Differentiated Support through Teacher Evaluation

Differentiating support for individual teachers requires the principal to engage in ongoing evaluation of teachers' instructional performance to identify their specific needs. Teacher evaluation typically involves a combination of ongoing and cumulative actions leading to an annual evaluation (Glickman et al., 2018).

A teacher professional growth plan (TPGP) is one tool that principals can utilize to develop a teacher's knowledge and instructional practice. An advantage of the TPGP is that teachers tend to be more invested in a plan where they develop their own goals for professional growth. Principals guide the development of the TPGP goals based on evaluative data collected through classroom observations and other supervisory practices. Teacher goals should be linked to student data and instructional practices that will improve student learning objectives (SLOs). Specific goals are outlined in the plan along with a time line for implementation.

The principal should meet periodically with the teacher to review progress with the plan. Benefits of the TPGPs for teachers include increased focus, responsibility for their own PD, reflective behavior, collegiality, and self-efficacy (Fenwick, 2004). The plans also provide unique opportunities for the principal to establish collaborative relationships with teachers. Trust between the principal and the teachers plays a role in the successful implementation of the TPGP. In order for teachers to feel comfortable in revealing potential weaknesses in their teaching, it is essential that they trust the process and their principal.

In the case where a teacher is uncooperative or unmotivated to improve her performance, the principal may develop a formal improvement plan to address specific shortcomings in the teacher's practices. While the intent of an improvement plan is similar to the TPGP in providing specific support and PD to improve teacher performance, it can lead to more consequential results regarding teacher employment. The improvement plan may also provide documentation for decisions leading to the nonrenewal of a teacher's continued employment if improvement in teaching performance does not occur (Glickman et al., 2018; Zepeda, 2016).

Providing Feedback

Just as it is important for teachers to provide students with feedback for growth, feedback is important in helping teachers improve their instruction; both of these feedback processes impact student learning. Teachers expect principals to provide them with timely and honest feedback and want principals to involve them in decision-making and collaborate with them in the instructional planning (Ozdemir & Sahin, 2020). In addition, teachers expect principals to remain objective and reward achievements.

However, teacher evaluations historically do not correlate to a change in teacher instructional practice because, typically, teachers do not receive the feedback they need and PD is not aligned with their areas of need (Marzano, 2009; Zepeda, 2016). Providing timely feedback can be challenging to principals who undoubtedly have complex responsibilities. However, principals must think of feedback as part of the teacher evaluation process and develop strategies to provide teachers feedback.

Principals can facilitate timely and effective feedback to teachers related to a number of activities, including classroom observations, team walkthroughs, and data team meetings (Gordon & Espinoza, 2020; Grissom et al., 2021). Effective feedback incorporates the following characteristics: it is goal-oriented, realistic, explicit, accentuates the positive, and is timely.

Even experienced principals can find it challenging to provide corrective feedback to teachers, so they may provide feedback that is overly positive or vague (Borders et al., 2017). Training principals to provide effective corrective feedback involves "a three-pronged approach: teach the skills, help shape delivery to the individual supervisee, and assist supervisors in getting past their reluctance" (Borders et al., 2017, p. 220).

When conveying difficult feedback, the principal should strive to be honest, clear, and direct with the teacher. In addition, the principal should encourage the teacher to reflect on the feedback and identify a realistic goal of improvement. Finally, throughout the conversation it is important for the principal to listen to the teacher's perspective and be prepared to offer appropriate support. Following these guidelines will help support a trusting and productive rapport between the principal and the teacher.

Mentoring

The principal as the instructional leader has the unique opportunity and responsibility of fostering the development of teachers as adult learners through targeted support that is based on building trusting relationships. Mentoring teachers is a strategy a principal can utilize to support the professional growth of teachers by facilitating thoughtful reflection of instructional practices.

Mentoring can build the instructional capacity of teachers and is especially important in providing support to new teachers to help them successfully navigate through their first year of teaching (Munir & Amin, 2020). Principals may also use mentoring as a strategy to support marginal teachers by pairing them with a more experienced teacher or coach. Mentoring teachers encourages the "assimilation of knowledge created between coaches and leaders on shared tasks and objectives," and, therefore, strengthens shared leadership among teacher leaders and the principal (Halpern et al., 2020, p. 670).

Mentoring is more likely to positively impact a teacher's performance if mentors are appropriately trained and matched to teachers. Additionally, the principal must provide adequate time and access for the mentor and teacher to meet on a regular basis. Although it is not always possible, assigning a mentor from the same grade level or subject area improves accessibility and the likelihood of shared or common responsibilities.

Building trust between a mentor and teacher involves clear communication between the mentor and teacher regarding their goals and expectations (Manning, Sheehy, & Ceballos, 2020). Principals can alleviate apprehension regarding the process, by specifically identifying the information that will be shared with the principal and any information that needs to be kept confidential between the mentor and the teacher. The principal should periodically follow up with the mentor and the teacher to ensure that the interactions are productive.

Monitoring Planning and Reviewing Instructional Plans

Providing additional time for collaborative planning does not in itself guarantee improving teachers' capacity for planning quality instruction. Monitoring the planning process and reviewing instructional plans is a crucial function of the principal as an instructional leader. Monitoring these processes reinforces the principal's expectations that adequate content support is provided using assessment data, setting appropriate goals, identifying key activities, and evaluating student progress (Sparks, 2018).

Principals, or their designee, must review lesson plans and provide feedback to teachers to ensure that lessons reflect data-driven decisions in relation to their school improvement goals. If a designee performs this task, the principal must be informed of the progress and areas of need. McTighe (2021) encourages principals to also review units of study to ensure that instructional planning revolves around big ideas including "enduring understandings, essential questions and performance assessment tasks" (p. 27).

> The classroom observations drive the amount of time I spend on lesson plans. Great teachers know how much time they need to put into their lesson plan. If a classroom observation demonstrates lack of planning, I ask the individual teacher to provide more thorough lesson plans for a period of time until the classroom observations demonstrate improvement. (C. Woods, personal communication, November 2021)

McTighe (2021) suggests that principals use the following "look-fors" when reviewing plans: a focus on priority content standards, communication to students of the learning goals, how goals will be assessed, alignment of instruction to the unit goals, active engagement with content and skills, embedded opportunities for students to receive timely and specific feedback, and summative assessments of the learning goals.

Principals use a variety of methods to monitor lesson plans and provide feedback to teachers that ranges in intensity:

> At the beginning of the year, we provide expectations for what teachers must include in their plans. Then, we provide feedback after the second week of school. From there, all teachers are required to post their lesson plans either inside their door or electronically. As we conduct walkthroughs and formal observations, we review the lesson plans to ensure that they are following expectations for lesson structure, standards, pacing, differentiation, and intervention. (J. White, personal communication, November 2021)

Classroom Observation

The purpose of classroom observations is to improve the quality of teaching and learning; however, O'Leary and Gewessler (2014) found that most teachers perceive classroom observations as stressful and ultimately not helpful in improving their instruction. Therefore, the principal should make classroom observations productive and part of school culture.

Principals train observers to conduct effective observation, reflection, feedback and feed-forward. While feedback relates to what happened during an observation, feed-forward is a process to help develop teachers by setting goals for future teaching (O'Leary & Gewessler, 2014). Additional characteristics of effective observations include providing teacher autonomy in determining the focus of observations and using a differentiated approach to observation that matches teachers' individual strengths and areas for improvement.

Developing trust is a key component of observations so teachers accept the process as helpful to their craft and feel encouraged to take risks. Trust within the observation process occurs when the observer facilitates reflection in a nonjudgmental manner. Principal M. Keith "affirms the things they are doing well and offers suggestions for ways to bump up a lesson" (personal communication, November 2021). When teachers perceive principal observations as a method of inquiry versus evaluation, they are more open to reflection, action research, and collaboration.

RECOMMENDATIONS FOR GROWTH

The following recommendations summarize the key teaching practices that encourage collaboration, reflection, and development of teacher instructional practices.

Develop a Strategic Plan for Developing Teachers

Developing a strategic plan to identify your school's high priority academic needs is a first step in determining how to support the specific needs of teachers and students (Glickman et al., 2018; Marzano, 2009; Miles & Frank, 2008). The plan should provide opportunities for collaboration and PD to target specific areas of need. A variety of resources are available to guide the strategic planning, such as the Strategic School Resource Diagnostic Tool, which asks questions such as, "How well does your school organize it's time, resources and talents?" (Miles & Frank, 2008, p.159).

Support PLCs

A PLC promotes collaborative and reflective inquiry. The principal supports the PLC by communicating a schoolwide focus based on student data as well as providing unencumbered time for teams of teachers to meet (Glickman et al., 2018). Principals also determine the various configurations of the PLC teams based on the needs of the schools. PLCs are structured around grade levels, subject areas, vertical teams across grades or content, or the entire faculty. The principals establish norms of trust and authentic reflective practice through modeling their own reflective behavior (Grissom et al., 2021).

Provide Opportunities for Teacher Leadership

A principal should examine both the academic goals of the school along with the individual strengths and talents of teachers to provide opportunities for leadership responsibilities (DuFour & Marzano, 2009). Teacher leaders lead change and influence other teachers to improve instructional practices (Gewertz, 2021; Halpern et al., 2021; Solvason & Kingston, 2020). Some examples of leadership opportunities that principals may utilize include leading PLC meetings or other groups, chairing special projects such as family engagement activities, facilitating school-based workshops, or leading book studies.

Differentiate the Supervision of Teachers

The PD needs of teachers are diverse across schools and, therefore, require principals to differentiate the type of support provided for individual teachers (Glickman et al., 2018). Teachers and the principal should analyze student data to develop appropriate SLOs. The SLOs are then aligned with other data sources, such as classroom observations, so that the principal can guide each teacher to develop their personalized TPGP (Glickman et al., 2018; Zepeda, 2016).

Encourage Collaboration between Teachers

Collaboration is at the heart of instructional supervision and is interwoven into many processes (Gordon & Espinoza, 2020). The principal influences the degree to which collaboration occurs throughout the school organization by ensuring that time and resources to support collaboration are adequately allocated.

Mentoring new or marginal teachers is a collaborative strategy to strengthen teacher performance (Halpern et al., 2020). Principals need to select master teachers who have the training and skill to effectively support teachers as mentors (Manning et al., 2020).

Collaborative lesson planning between teachers is another important way that principals can support collegial relationships between teachers (Goodwin, 2012; Mathews, 2011).

Observations

Classroom observations are another tool for principals and teachers to collaborate and improve instructional delivery. Principals develop appropriate criteria for observations based on teacher and student needs and feedback must always be given to teachers in a nonthreatening manner. Observations should be viewed as a tool for growth and collaborative discussion.

Instructional rounds, another form of observation, provide a unique opportunity for principals to promote collaboration and reflection between groups of teachers (Marzano, 2011). This interactive process helps teachers to examine their own instructional practices and a forum to explore new strategies within a trusting and reflective environment.

Develop a Plan for Your PD

There is no doubt that the principal has an impact on teaching and learning through their supervisory actions. Effective instructional leaders understand the value of participating in PD opportunities alongside teachers (Glickman et al., 2018; Ozdemir & Sahin, 2020; Zepeda, 2016). Authentic participation in collaborative activities such as PLCs, collaborative planning, and instructional rounds communicates to teachers that the principal values these activities. In addition, principals should engage in a self-assessment to determine areas of their supervisory skills that can benefit from additional training.

SUMMARY

Principals who implement effective instructional supervisory practices improve instruction and student achievement (Glickman et al., 2018; Zepeda, 2016). Supervisory characteristics that support this include building collaborative relationships with teachers, creating a trust-based climate that encourages experimentation and risk-taking, and synergizing individual and team efforts (Marzano, 2011; Ozdemir & Shain, 2020). Principals accomplish this by embedding PD that is differentiated based on both student and teacher needs (Glickman et al., 2018).

In addition, the principal supports collaborative inquiry that encourages teachers to examine their instructional practices around student achievement. This reflective inquiry occurs in both formal and informal settings (Grissom et al., 2021; Kempen & Steyn, 2017). These supervisory processes occur across the organization with the understanding that supervision is an ongoing and long-term process that is based on focused and strategic planning to intentionally align data, resources, and practices to develop teachers' knowledge and instructional practices (DuFour & Marzano, 2009).

Instructional leaders use a shared, or distributive, style of leadership that utilizes the strengths of individual teachers and provides opportunities to develop leadership skills in teachers (DuFour & Marzano, 2009). Delegating responsibilities motivates and encourages teachers to actively improve instructional practices, take risks, and engage in action research (Gewertz, 2021; Halpern et al., 2021; Solvason & Kingston, 2020).

Principals impact instructional practices by providing extended periods of time for teachers to collaborate in PLC meetings, lesson planning meetings, and embedded PD. The principal and leadership team build trust and collegial relationships by actively participating in these collaborative meetings.

Monitoring classroom instruction and teacher evaluation are important functions of the instructional leader (Glickman et al., 2018; Marzano, 2009; Zepeda, 2016). Principals set expectations for teachers regarding lesson plans and instructional practices and then follow up with frequent formal and informal classroom observations; timely and specific feedback is provided by the principal and other designated supervisors to the teacher to help guide instruction (Borders et al., 2017).

Instructional supervision is based on the tenet of increasing student learning through the improvement of teacher practices (Glickman et al., 2018; Marzano, 2009). Therefore, the support provided to teachers is differentiated based on the specific needs of both teachers and students (Zepeda, 2016). Instructional supervision supports a growth mindset and support for teachers may include developing a TPGP, mentoring, observing, or participating in instructional rounds (Marzano, 2009; Ozdemir & Shain, 2020).

REFLECTION QUESTIONS

1. What would a strategic plan for developing the teachers at your school include? What strategies could you use to develop teacher leaders? Discuss how you differentiate support that the teachers receive. How do you support marginal teachers?

2. How do you foster collaboration between teachers? What is your expectation for collaborative planning? How can you encourage teachers to reflect on their instructional practices?
3. How will you monitor teaching and learning? How do you use classroom observations to improve teaching? How could you provide effective feedback?
4. What PD or resources do you need to improve your supervisory skills?

REFERENCES

Baker, J. A., & Bloom, G. S. (2017). Growing support for principals: Principal supervisors collaborate and problem solve in learning communities. *Learning Professional, 38*(2), 61–65.

Borders, L. D., Welfare, L. E., Sackett, C. R., & Cashwell, C. (2017). New supervisors' struggles and successes with corrective feedback. *Counselor Education & Supervision, 56*(3), 208–24.

Costa, A. L., Garmston, R. Hayes, C., & Ellison, J. (2015). *Cognitive coaching: Developing self-directed leaders and learners.* Third Edition. New York: Rowman & Littlefield.

Danielson, C. (2007). The many faces of leadership. *Educational Leadership, 65*(1), 14–19.

DuFour, R., & Marzano, R. J. (2009). High-leverage strategies for principal leadership. *Educational Leadership, 66*(5), 62–68.

Fenwick, T. J. (2004). Teacher learning and professional growth plans: Implementation of a provincial policy. *Journal of Curriculum and Supervision, 19*(3), 250–82.

Gewertz, C. (2021). Where teachers take the lead on science curriculum. *Education Week, 40*(22), 10–13.

Glickman, C. D., Gordon, S. P., & Ross-Gordon, J. M. (2018). *Supervision and instructional leadership: A developmental approach.* Tenth Edition. New York: Pearson.

Goodwin, B. (2012). New teachers face three common challenges. *Educational Leadership, 69*(8), 84–85.

Gordon, S. P., & Espinoza, S. (2020). Instructional supervision for culturally responsive teaching. *Educational Considerations, 45*(3), 1–22.

Grissom, J. A., Egalite, A. J., & Lindsay, C. A. (2021). What great principals really do. *Educational Leadership, 78*(7), 21–25.

Halpern, C., Szecsi, T., & Mak, V. (2021). "Everyone can be a leader": Early childhood education leadership in a center serving culturally and linguistically diverse children and families. *Early Childhood Education Journal, 49*(4), 669–79.

Hirsh, S., & Crow, T. (2017). Tying it altogether: Becoming a learning team: A guide to a teacher-led cycle of continuous improvement. *Learning Professional, 38*(5), 58–66.

Honig, M., & Rainey, L. (2020). A teaching-and-learning approach to principal supervision. *Phi Delta Kappan, 102*(20), 54–57.

Kempen, M. E., & Steyn, G. M. (2017). An investigation of teacher's collaborative learning in a continuous professional development program in South African special schools. *Journal of Asian and African Studies, 52*(2), 157–71.

Leithwood, K., & Strauss, T. (2009). Turnaround schools: Leadership lessons. *Education Canada, 49*(2), 26–29.

Manning, T., Sheehy, K., & Ceballos, L. (2020). Making mentoring work online. *Learning Professional, 41*(4), 56–58.

Marzano, R. J. (2011). Making the most of instructional rounds. *Educational Leadership, 68*(5), 80–81.

McTighe, J. (2021). For school leaders, reviewing isolated lessons isn't enough: Evaluators need to consider lessons in the context of the overall curriculum unit, like the parts of a full-course meal. *Educational Leadership, 78*(9), 26–28.

Miles, K. H., & Frank, S. (2008). *The strategic school: Making the most of people, time, and money.* California: Corwin Press.

Munir, F., & Amin, M. (2020). Head teachers' perceptions about mentoring practices in primary schools. *Bulletin of Education & Research, 42*(3), 131–46.

O'Leary, M. & Gewessler, A. (2014). Changing the culture: Beyond graded lesson observation. *Adult Learning, 25*(3), 38–41.

Ozdemir, G., & Sahin, S. (2020). Principal's supervisory practices for teacher professional development: Bureaucratic and professional perspectives. *International Online Journal of Educational Sciences, 12*(1), 18–36.

Solvason, C., & Kingston, A. (2020). How subject leader collaborations across schools can act as a source of personal and curriculum development. *Curriculum and Teaching Dialogue, 22*(1), 91–106.

Sparks, S. D. (2018). Tinkering toward a better education system. *Education Week, 37*(20), 1–16.

St. Clair, S. (2020). Accentuate the positive: Redefine coaching to support teachers and alleviate stress. *Principal, 100*(1), 26.

Westberry, L. A. (2020). *Putting the pieces together: A systems approach to school leadership.* Lanham, MD: Rowman & Littlefield.

Wiggins, G., & McTighe, J. (2005). *Understanding by design.* Second Edition. Upper Saddle River, NJ: Prentice Hall.

Zepeda, Sally J. (2016). Principals' perspectives: Professional learning and marginal teachers on formal plans of improvement. *Research in Educational Administration & Leadership, 1*(1), 25–59.

Chapter Eight

From Having All the Answers to Engaging in Collective Learning

Reenvisioning the Role of the Principal and the Approach to Support

Paula Tharp, Myron B. Labat, and Leigh A. McMullan, Mississippi State University

INTRODUCTION

The findings of a survey by the National Association of Secondary School Principals released on December 8, 2021, have issued an urgent call to the field. An astounding 38 percent of the principals report that they plan to leave the profession in the next three years. Underneath this statistic were the following:

- When asked about support received from central office, only 25 percent of the principals "strongly agree" that the support they receive meets their needs.
- Only 23 percent of the principals "strongly agree" that they receive adequate support from the school district to advance student learning.
- Additionally, 77 percent would like to have more opportunities to connect with the principals facing the same issues and challenges (National Association of Secondary School Principals [NASSP], 2021).

Principal preparation programs, policymakers, and school system supporters must take heed. What would adequate support for principals to advance student learning look like? How can the field, from preparation programs to on-the-job supports provide opportunities for principals to address their needs and challenges? Further, how can leadership preparation programs for principals and district leaders contribute to their success after graduation?

The authors of this chapter, faculty of an educational leadership program engaged in continuous improvement of a principal preparation program, have spent the year prior to publication in partnership with a school district assessing the challenges candidates face after graduation, the source of those stressors and challenges, and how district personnel, who would support them at every stage of their career, might begin to better address them.

In leadership preparation programs, faculty observes the candidates' beliefs upon graduation and entry into the principalship that they are expected to have all the answers, lest they be seen as inadequate or unprepared. For acting principals, this belief may contribute to working harder to hide the idea that they do not have all the answers rather than seeking assistance from others to learn what they do not yet know. Based on this understanding and lessons learned, the educational leadership faculty authoring this chapter has begun to consider how to better support principals by replacing the pressure to *know* with the imperative to continuously *learn*.

The second concern of the faculty is while the conception of the principalship has evolved significantly in the accountability age, the training and preparation for central office actors who supervise principals may still lag behind, as evidenced by the Wallace Foundation Principal Supervisor Initiative (PSI), aimed at shifting the role of principal supervisors from operational to instructional leadership support (Goldring et al., 2020). During the accountability age, educational stakeholders, communities, and policymakers have begun to focus on student outcomes in relation to principal effectiveness.

This evolution has seen a gradual, yet significant, shift away from principals as building managers to principal effectiveness being tied directly to student outcomes. Consistent with this effort, the PSI sought to assist districts in transforming the role of the principal supervisor from one of administration, compliance, and management to one focused on instructional support of principals. The PSI approached this transformation in districts by

- altering the job description of principal supervisors to one primarily focused on instructional support;
- reducing the supervisor's scope of control;
- improving the supervisor's capacity to support principals through training;
- developing a succession plan for new supervisors; and
- reinforcing the central office structure to support the changes to the supervisor role.

Altering the role of the principal supervisor resulted in a shift to how supervisors spent their day, which was a start in shifting the way they support principals instructionally (Goldring et al., 2020, p. xv).

Not surprisingly, the pressure for principals to appear competent at every turn coupled with an amplified focus on accountability for student outcomes and a dearth of meaningful support from central office has resulted in a significant increase in the level of pressure and stress of the job (NASSP, 2021). With many principals' jobs and livelihoods being tied directly to student achievement, principals have found themselves feeling more and more alone in the role (Bauer, Silver, & Schwartzer, 2019), with decisions they make in terms of hiring, instructional initiatives, and curriculum having far-reaching implications.

To provide for both principals and the central office actors who would ideally support their success, the faculty embarked on a multiyear partnership with a district leader focused on reframing improvement as a learning challenge for every role group within the system. Specifically, the P–12 educational leadership department and district official worked together to make progress on a shared developmental framework to achieve a common goal.

Using vignettes to illustrate specific lessons learned to date, the authors share how this visionary leader in partnership with the educational leadership faculty is using the principles of the Internal Coherence (IC) Framework (Forman, Stosich, & Bocala, 2017) and its developmental trajectory to grow principal efficacy, agency, and a willingness to engage candidly in shared learning experiences for the purpose of professional growth. Additionally, the authors will share examples of how the superintendent in the same district is structuring the work of those who support principals in an effective and productive way.

Forman et al. (2017) define IC as "the collective capability of the adults in a school building or an educational system to connect and align resources to carry out an improvement strategy" (p. 3). By using the research-based and theory-driven approach outlined in the IC Framework, the superintendent has been able to identify the specific structures, processes, resources, and ongoing learning experiences needed to provide for all the practitioners in this system.

Further, by embracing the IC tenet, school improvement is a challenge of adult learning rather than compliance (Forman et al., 2017); the superintendent is fostering an environment and a culture in which principals are encouraged to be learners alongside the system actors learning to effectively support them. Shared highlights include experiences with three levels of the system: the superintendent, the district principals, and the district's team of instructional coaches, all of which shine a light on the need to reframe the traditional expectations *of* school leaders and supports provided *for* them.

AN UNTENABLE PROPOSITION

Despite the relatively recent emphasis on academic outcomes, other responsibilities that come along with the job have not diminished. Principals are asked to spend the bulk of their day engaged in behaviors directly impacting student outcomes, yet the other duties important for a school to run smoothly must be managed as well. Studies examining the stresses and pressures of the principalship reiterate this point indicating that principals find themselves torn between focusing on school improvement, student outcomes, test scores, teacher development, and the daily challenges of the job (Huang, Hochbein, & Simons, 2018).

According to Superville (2019), nearly half of new principals leave their positions after only three years in the role, and nearly 20 percent leave every year. Recent studies suggest that principal effectiveness is a factor in determining whether principals leave their schools. Principals who are found to be less effective as measured by teacher perceptions and evaluation instruments are more likely to leave their roles (Grissom & Bartanen, 2019).

Additionally, principals are more likely to leave schools with less resources than they are to leave schools with ample resources (Loeb, Kalogrides, & Horng, 2010; Tekleselassie & Choi, 2019). This reality disproportionately impacts high-poverty schools and schools serving students of color (Béteille, Kalogrides, & Loeb, 2012; DeAngelis & White, 2011; Fuller & Young, 2009; Gates et al., 2006; Loeb et al., 2010). Given how critical the role of the principal is to student learning (Leithwood et al., 2004), the call to reenvision principal expectations and support could not be clearer.

The next three vignettes from the partnership illustrate the critical shifts suggested to the way system leaders and universities currently support principals. The vignettes chronicle how one thoughtful and committed system leader is reframing support for principals by understanding the challenges in terms of a knowledge gap, providing the structure and processes for shared learning as a role group, and distributing responsibility for improving student outcomes away from principals alone to other actors in the system.

The experiences offer guidance to those who would support principals by acknowledging (1) the need for a concrete and shared theory of action for how the work actually gets done; (2) the recognition that the complex, developmental nature of improving student achievement requires principals to learn rather than know; and (3) the recognition that it is not principals alone who can solve the problem of student achievement but that it is a common challenge in which each role group bears responsibility for a strategic piece of the puzzle (Forman et al. 2017).

Lesson 1: Lean into the Knowledge Gap

The superintendent saw the value of the constructs that the IC Framework could bring to improvement efforts in his struggling, high-poverty rural district (Forman et al., 2017). Originally designed as an actionable roadmap for school leaders, the framework spells out specifically what leaders would need to do in their buildings to move the needle on student learning.

Research has indicated that the instructional core and the academic task are the drivers of what students ultimately learn (Cohen & Ball, 1999; Doyle, 1983). The IC framework uses a reverse approach to the learning experiences teachers would require to deepen the level of the tasks they provide for students. It also outlines the implications for principals as the orchestrator of the ongoing adult learning experiences (professional development, teacher teams) that the faculty would need (see Figure 8.1).

"This should be the accountability model in our district," was the superintendent's first reaction to the model (anonymous, personal communication, November 13, 2020). Convinced of the logic of the approach, he determined that he would hold his principals accountable for the components outlined in the framework, including the creation of a vision for instructional practice, a culture of psychological safety for adult learning, and teacher teams capable of engaging in constructive conflict and productive debate.

The model's explicit focus on psychological safety for shared and public learning (Edmonson, 1999) and the growth of individual and collective efficacy (Goddard & Goddard, 2001) beliefs for instructional improvement particularly resonated with him. Determined to effect substantial improvement

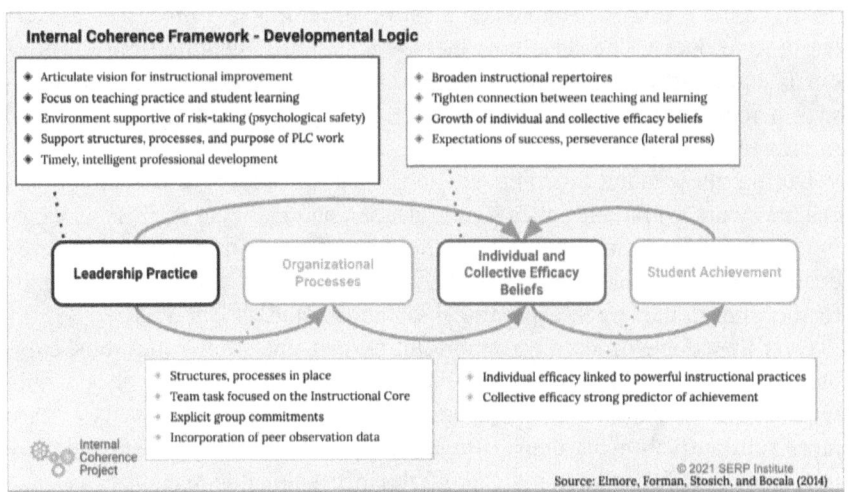

Figure 8.1. IC Framework Developmental Logic

in the service of students, the superintendent's first order of business was to replace the culture of compliance-driven decision-making and low expectations for student performance with a district culture in which everyone, from students to teachers to principals to his own leadership team, were required to bring their intellectual A game each and every day.

The superintendent used the opportunity of introducing the framework to highlight his hope that principals would engage in independent thinking and risk-taking and publicly voice their ideas, questions, and needs. However, when encouraging principals to provide feedback on using IC as a strategy, they either were silent or supported the superintendent's ideas without question. Despite sincere attempts to "empower" this group, his intuitive sense for creating a psychologically safe (Edmonson, 1999) setting for discourse, and his explicit verbal permission to challenge his own ideas, principals remained hesitant to engage.

The first lesson learned for the superintendent in the context of the partnership was that increasing agency to contribute ideas required not only permission but a level of knowledge and skill his principals did not yet have. Cultivating a cadre of principals willing to actively voice ideas or challenge the status quo required him to create the learning opportunities that the principals need to develop their thinking and structure their input.

Too often educators sidestep the role of knowledge in, ironically, the field of education and frame the challenge of improving student outcomes at scale as one that can be solved with mandates, or, in this case, encouragement to speak up. For this superintendent, his first shift in approach was recognizing that growing agency begins with growing understanding. To do so, he promptly established a set of structures and processes for this learning to occur. The structures include a standing meeting time for principals and instructional coaches, and joint learning sessions for both teams with a focus on creating a system-wide theory of action for instructional improvement.

During these adult learning sessions, school leaders and instructional coaches work with their colleagues to deepen and calibrate their understanding on key IC constructs, such as the role of an instructional vision, the qualities it must have to shine a light on the work of teacher teams, or its relationship to the larger, aspirational vision for student learning.

Over the course of learning opportunities, principals raise questions, comparing research to current practice, and consider what support they would request of the instructional coaches or the superintendent as they learn more substantively what their instructional improvement challenge entailed. Instructional coaches learn more about the instructional core and task (Cohen & Ball, 1999), develop common processes for working to support principals, calibrate their understanding of valued student capacities, and plan strategies to address the learning needs of teacher teams.

Further, the superintendent has worked to reframe improvement as a challenge of ongoing learning by explicitly requesting permission to participate in IC sessions as a learner himself. In so doing, he is growing psychological safety for everyone in the district to *not* act as though they have all the answers. As they collectively deepen their knowledge, the superintendent is coming to dispel the notion that principals alone have all the answers as well as dispelling the notion of principals as solely accountable for student learning gains.

Lesson 2: Push for Depth and Clarity—Not Pretty Words

Having set the stage to prioritize opportunities for principals to learn, the superintendent is pushing for principals to make their thinking more robust, concrete, and research-based. The strategy is also addressing the desire for more time to learn together with peers that is expressed by the principals (NASSP, 2021). Having this set-aside time to learn together allows for a safe space for the principals to engage with challenging material without the presence of those they supervise (teachers, instructional leadership team) or their district supervisors.

During this time, principals dive deeper into how a school leader moves a school from the current state to the desired state. Principals think together about the developmental process of improvement, action steps for moving a school, the impact of action steps, and focusing on the instructional core (Cohen & Ball, 1999). It is anticipated that over time this more solid understanding will lead to the principals' increased agency desired by the superintendent, efficacy for continuous improvement, and increased capacity to facilitate teachers' learning, ultimately resulting in improved student outcomes (Goddard & Goddard, 2001).

The principal learning time is used to deepen and push the manner in which principals traditionally talk about their work. For example, the principals in the group are clearly internalizing ideas that filter down from educational leadership research, including the importance of a vision, effective teams, productive climates, and student voice. However, how these constructs are envisioned to lead to improvements in student outcomes is not yet known as demonstrated in the following example.

When discussing improvement areas of focus, principals easily discussed the importance of working with teams, reviewing data, and working with nonproficient students. When pressed for more explanation, principals' responses suggested that understanding of how well-known practices of good leaders (vision, teams, culture, curriculum) actually interrelate, interconnect, and interact to ultimately translate into schoolwide improvement in student outcomes was less clear. When pressed to discuss interconnectivity of practices, principals struggled to articulate why the interconnectivity leads to improved student outcomes.

The theory supporting the IC Framework, alternatively, challenged principals to move beyond the *what*, and instead, challenged them to think together about the *how* and the *why* of focusing on key constructs including shared adult learning. To illustrate, principals readily voiced the importance of having teachers work together in teams and professional learning communities—the *what*. They quickly talked about teams that are "rocking n' and rolling." However, when pressed to discuss what they mean by "rocking n' and rolling" and *why* working productively in teacher teams leads to improved student outcomes, principals struggled.

Principals easily discussed increasing and improving collaboration, comradery, motivation, willingness to come to work, planning together, and talking together to get to know the whole child. This surface-level discussion was comfortable and free-flowing. When principals were asked to say more about the *how* and *why* of collaboration, comradery, and motivation by completing the following stem, there was pause.

> IF we do everything we articulate, THEN teachers will, . . . which will result in students who . . . which will attain the student outcomes we desire by. . .

In order to move teacher team meetings from suggestion-sharing sessions to productive interdependent learning sessions, leading to substantive and coherent changes in teaching and learning, principals must understand how to facilitate the shift and why the approach will ultimately result in increased teacher effectiveness and improved student learning. They must understand the process and the value of building coherence (Forman et al., 2017) and collective efficacy (Goddard & Goddard, 2001). If principals are to come to understand, supporters of principals and university preparation faculty must as well.

A lesson learned by the facilitators of principal discussion was that principals in the partnership were not yet ready with the confidence—the efficacy and agency—necessary to talk substantively about what it would take for them to act as facilitators of teacher learning and learners alongside their teachers (Goddard & Goddard, 2001) rather than simply providing the structure and time for teachers to meet.

According to Cohen and Ball (1999), "A second explanation for the typically small effects of school improvement interventions is that most are not designed to provide the opportunities for teacher learning that would be needed to change classroom instruction" (p. 1). Without substantive shared learning among teachers, principals, and principal supporters, student outcomes will not likely improve.

The work of principals facilitating and learning alongside their teachers is developmental. This development includes instructional vision, team productivity, and capacity building (Forman et al., 2017).

Lesson 3: Spread Responsibility beyond Principals

Having reframed the role of the principal as learning to move a school following a collectively understood theory of action, the superintendent was able to devote the work of other system actors to this shared project. The superintendent began by assigning the district's instructional coaches the responsibility of supporting principals in their progress along the IC developmental trajectory, acknowledging the disciplinary expertise required to improve instruction and the bandwidth of principals already charged with so many things.

This was accomplished initially by shifting their role description from a group of individual coaches assigned to specific schools to a team of district experts engaged in the joint work of achieving improved student outcomes in preschool through twelfth grade. In similar fashion to the principal learning strand, the superintendent created a weekly learning session for the team to explore *their role* in bringing the tenets of the IC Framework to life in schools across the district.

During weekly learning sessions, the coaching team digs more deeply into IC constructs aligned with their expertise. According to the IC Framework, all of the collaboration and professional development in a school building are in service of a vision for the instructional core (Cobb et al., 2018; Cohen & Ball, 1999). In contrast to a traditional vision statement focused on desired outcomes, a vision for the core articulates the principles of the interactions among teachers, students, and instructional materials theorized to generate the student learning outcomes that the district seeks.

Further, creating a vision for the core requires the instructional coaching team to engage with research on the constructs of the instructional core and academic task (Doyle, 1983) to consider together the nature of the interactions they currently see in classrooms districtwide. This also encourages them to pool their pedagogical and disciplinary expertise around desired student learning outcomes and the classroom interactions required to generate them.

Aligning the work of this team to the core work of school leaders also involved changing their role from those who coach individual teachers in response to a classroom observation to those who *teach* teams or entire faculty what they need to learn to reach a vision for the instructional core. To date, the instructional leadership team has worked to unpack what students would need to know, understand, and be able to do to rise to the district vision of deeply literate problem solvers.

The team was also able to apply this to the experiences students would need across classrooms to realize substantive learning goals to become deeply literate problem solvers. Pooling their collective thinking around the constructs of IC enabled the team to make their individual and internal expertise shared, explicit, and useful to support principals' work. From "I know good instruction when I see it" to creating a draft instructional vision, which explicitly states what will be happening in classrooms when desired student learning is achieved, this team created a resource critical for principals' work with their faculty.

The superintendent has also formalized a structure for ongoing collaboration among the district principals and the instructional leadership team. Goals for the collaborative structure include the opportunity for coaches to share resources, such as a draft vision for the core and giving principals the opportunity to weigh in, ask questions, or request further support.

Over time, the instructional coaches and district principals will calibrate their understanding of what needs to be happening in classrooms (vision for the core), what is currently happening in classrooms (current state), the goals for teacher learning required to make progress toward the vision, and the most high-leverage strategy for facilitating teachers gaining the requisite knowledge and skill. Principals and instructional leads will jointly create improvement strategies, determining the learning teachers need, and organizing the professional development or facilitated experiences on teacher teams by which teachers receive it.

Discussion and Implications

If the field is to support principals at the level required to address the rate of principals reporting dissatisfaction in their positions (NASSP, 2021), university faculty and central office personnel must come together as those who support principals and take seriously the call to examine and shift approaches. The charge begins with acceptance of the complexity of a principal's role and a serious look at what support is necessary to meet the needs of principals as they face the evolving challenges. Ultimately, any considerations for changes to how principals are supported should be made with an eye toward improving student outcomes.

The collaborative project herein discussed provides examples of working with several levels of the school system and discovering the disconnects. Principals and school system personnel have the metrics needed to improve teaching and learning. For example, school and district leaders know that teachers working effectively in teams are a desirable attribute of an effective school, however, principals and district supporters must have a clear pathway for moving the teams in place to productive learning groups.

The clear implication is that robust support must be keenly focused on the needs of the adults within the system to identify where the knowledge gaps lie (Forman, Knecht, & Fray-Oliver, 2020) and join with principals and other building-level leaders to determine how to move teacher learning teams from surface-level conversation to more substantive and interdependent learning teams sharply focused on improving student outcomes.

Implications for the Field: Recommendations for Critical Shifts

Observing how progress is accelerating as barriers are removed and school leaders' willingness to admit when they *did not know* is becoming more normalized, university faculty and system leadership are seeing shared responsibility for improvement increase across system levels. As a result, the critical shift recommended for those who support principals is to lean into the knowledge gap creating safe settings for all system-level players to acknowledge areas of needed support.

At the central office level, leaning into the knowledge gap suggests an acknowledgment that it is not the principal alone who should have all the answers to challenges and barriers of school improvement. This shift may signal a new way of working for central office support personnel. In addition, leaning into the knowledge gap at the university level means a shift for educational leadership faculty to focus more on preparing candidates to be honest and transparent leaders without feeling insecure about their leadership knowledge and abilities.

One way to counter the mindset of "knowing" is shifting the culture of how school leadership and school improvement is viewed and conceptualized. "Improvement is a challenge of learning, not implementation" (Elmore, 1996; Forman et al., 2017, p. 7) is a statement that embodies the essence of this powerful shift in thinking with the potential for substantial impact to the education profession.

Envisioning leadership through a shared and continuous learning (Marks & Printy, 2003) philosophy is another critical shift in designing evidence-based supports for principals. A primary takeaway from the project between the educational leadership faculty and the school district is that viewing learning as a shared process where all involved parties are engaged at different levels may be helpful in removing the stigma of not knowing and instead may serve to foster a culture of shared responsibility for improvement.

Further, in the philosophical approach of shared and continuous learning, the principal is positioned as part of the leadership team working with others to seek solutions that will improve student outcomes. In addition, improvement is seen as an ongoing learning experience with continuous consideration given to what adults need to know and be able to do to meet the contextual challenges of improvement. This continuous and shared learning model removes some of the pressure from the principal to have all the solutions and shifts it to more of a team approach to problem-solving.

This philosophy can and should be explored at the building level as well in relation to principals working with faculty. The approach highlights a shared focus on problem-solving rather than a top-down approach wherein the principal seeks the solutions and disseminates the resulting directives to the faculty. The top-down approach leaves the principal isolated, without engagement from teachers, and does little to take advantage of the vast knowledge and perspectives held by the faculty.

If districts can successfully transition from an isolated learning approach in favor of a shared learning philosophy, it could help in accelerating substantial professional growth among its leaders, thereby better positioning the district for improvement. In the process, the district is likely to see increased capacity and efficacy among teacher leaders. Facilitating more growth and responsibility among teacher leaders can only serve to strengthen the overall mission and vision of the district.

In their work developing systems of professional learning, Forman et al. (2020) describe the concept "Throughline of Learning," in which the model highlights the instructional core and focuses on the idea that system-wide shared adult learning is necessary if school districts are to reimagine how they approach instructional improvement. They further describe how this focus on ongoing shared learning experiences builds on recent research and has implications for greater improvement (Forman et al., 2020).

A third critical shift in how we think of support for principals involves helping personnel in support roles parse out their greatest contribution to the support of the principals as well as processes and procedures for doing so. Previously discussed was how the superintendent came to realize what he needed to do to build agency in principals setting aside the structures and times for them to learn together.

It was further determined that expectations had to be established for how the instructional coaching team would work together as well as how they would work as an entity with principals to support improvement in the schools. The superintendent learned that there was a significant disconnect between the expectations or desired goals and what superintendent, the principals, and the instructional coaches needed to do in order to meet those expectations.

Lessons learned in studying the PSI (Goldring et al., 2018) may provide guidance in thinking about the best ways various system-level actors can provide support to principals. For example, recommendations brought forth by the PSI included narrowing the principal supervisor's scope of control to that of instructional support rather than general administration, changing the culture within the central office, and balancing the responsibilities of supervisors while also increasing the opportunities for training and professional development for supervisors.

While this approach may be fundamentally different from the way the role of the principal has traditionally been framed, it may be worth considering to both ease the enormous pressure placed on the principal and include others in the problem-solving process. Perhaps such structured support could also serve to assist in reducing the level of principal turnover that is ravaging the profession.

Additionally, by embracing the shared learning and leadership approach, greater focus is placed on building collective efficacy schoolwide as well as the individual efficacy of teachers and teacher leaders. According to Goddard, Hoy, and Hoy (2004), the connections between beliefs of collective efficacy and student achievement are dependent upon relationships among these collective efficacy beliefs, teacher self-efficacy, professional practice, and teacher's influence on decision-making related to instruction.

Implications for Principal Preparation Programs

Another important observation made through the partnership is that perhaps university educational leadership faculty should revisit their philosophy and approach to principal preparation. One major barrier to forward progress for the partner school district is working with principals to dispel the misconception that principals are expected to have all the answers.

Universities might be wise to consider other approaches to principal preparation that place the principal as one piece of the shared learning process rather than the purveyor of answers (Forman et al., 2020).

This may represent a significant shift from traditional approaches to educational leadership training and, thus, may require additional coursework or discussions to ensure leadership candidates have a clear understanding of this philosophy and the role they play in the improvement and problem-solving process. Having a clear philosophical understanding of this approach may be helpful in eliminating some of the traditional barriers new leaders and school districts have faced in the past.

SUMMARY

When looking at the impact that principals have on school success and student outcomes, it becomes quite evident that principal support is a critical area that central office leaders and universities should be directing their efforts to ensure that principals are well prepared for the challenges ahead. It is also important to note that support of principals begins at the candidate level when they are matriculating through principal preparation programs and ideally should continue well into their transition to a leadership assignment.

It may be wise for universities preparing candidates for leadership to approach preparation from a developmental perspective, wherein support continues beyond completion of the candidate's educational leadership degree. This may involve universities extending their partnership with the school district into the candidate's first or second year on the job.

Additionally, district leadership may consider approaching their support of principals with the same developmental philosophy, understanding that earning a leadership degree is not the end of a principal's development, but rather it is the beginning. The educational leadership faculty participating in this partnership have begun to undergo a philosophical shift in terms of how it views leadership preparation, placing the principal as part of a collective leadership team (working collaboratively with that team and the faculty) to uncover solutions rather than being the sole primary problem solver.

REFLECTION QUESTIONS

1. In addition to the proposed strategies for building principal leadership capacity, what other recommendations would you suggest for strengthening principal leadership capacity?
2. As described in the chapter, creating a culture where psychological safety is ensured allows the school leaders to feel comfortable in learning and growing among their peers. What other suggestions do you have for increasing the level of psychological safety for school leaders?
3. The authors propose reenvisioning the role of those who supervise principals, placing a greater focus on instructional support as opposed to administrative support. Describe other ways that you might improve the level of instructional support for principals.
4. Principal turnover has been a major concern in the field of educational leadership. What are some ways that you would propose addressing the rate of principal turnover?

5. The authors emphasize the importance of teacher leadership in improving the overall collective efficacy within a school or a district. What other ideas do you have for strengthening and improving collective efficacy within a school or a district?

REFERENCES

Bauer, S., Silver, L., & Schwartzer, J. (2019). The impact of isolation on new principals' persistence: Evidence from a southern US state. *Educational Management, Administration, & Leadership, 47*(3), 383–99.

Béteille, T., Kalogrides, D., & Loeb, S. (2012). Stepping stones: Principal career paths and school outcomes. *Social Science Research, 41*(4), 904–19. https://doi.org/10.1016/j.ssresearch.2012.03.003

Cobb, P., Jackson, K., Henrik, E, & Smith, T. (2018). *Systems for instructional improvement: creating coherence from the classroom to the district office*. Cambridge, MA: Harvard Education Press.

Cohen, D. K., & Ball, D. L. (1999). *Instruction, capacity, and improvement*. CPRE Research Report Series RR43. Philadelphia, PA: Consortium for Policy Research in Education, University of Pennsylvania.

DeAngelis, K. J., & White, B. R. (2011). *Principal turnover in Illinois public schools, 2001–2008* (Policy Research No. IERC 2011-1). Illinois Education Research Council.

Doyle, W. (1983). Academic work. *Review of Educational Research, 53*(2), 159–99.

Edmonson, A. (1999). Psychological safety and learning behavior in work teams. *Administrative Science Quarterly, 44*(2), 350–83.

Elmore, R. (1996). Getting to scale with good educational practice. *Harvard Educational Review, 66*(1), 1–26.

Forman, M. L., Knecht, D., & Fray-Oliver, T. (March 2020). *Becoming a system of professional learning: Conceptualizing improvement as a throughline of learning*. New York: Bank Street College of Education.

Forman, M. L., Stosich, E. L., & Bocala, C. (2017). *The internal coherence framework: Creating the conditions for continuous improvement in schools*. Cambridge, MA: Harvard Education Press.

Fuller, E. J., & Young, M. D. (2009). *Tenure and retention of newly hired principals in Texas*. University Council for Educational Administration, Department of Educational Administration, University of Texas at Austin.

Fusarelli, B., Fusarelli, L., & Riddick, F. (2018). Planning for the future: Leadership development and succession planning in education. *Journal of Research on Leadership Education, 13*(3), 286–313.

Gates, S. M., Ringel, J. S., Santibanez, L., Guarino, C., Ghosh-Dastidar, B., & Brown, A. (2006). Mobility and turnover among school principals. *Economics of Education Review, 25*(3), 289–302. https://doi.org/10.1016/j.econedurev.2005.01.008

Goddard, R. D. & Goddard, Y. L. (2001) A multilevel analysis of the relationship between teacher and collective efficacy in urban schools. *Teaching and Teacher Education, 17*, 807–18.

Goddard, R. D., Hoy, W. K., & Woolfolk Hoy, A. (2004). Collective efficacy beliefs: Theoretical developments, empirical evidence, and future directions. *Educational Researcher, 33*(3), 3–13.

Goldring, E. B., Grissom, J. A., Rubin, M., Rogers L. K., Neel, M., & Clark, M.A. (2018). *A new role emerges for principal supervisors: Evidence from six districts in the principal supervisor initiative.* Retrieved from https://www.wallacefoundation.org/knowledge-center/pages/a-new-role-emerges-for-principal-supervisors.aspx

Goldring, E. B., Clark, M. A., Rubin, M., Rogers, L. K., Grissom, J. A., Gill, B., Kautz, T., McCullough, M., Neel, M., & Burnett, A. (2020). *Changing the principal supervisor role to better support principals: Evidence from the Principal Supervisor Initiative.* The Wallace Foundation. Retrieved from https://www.wallacefoundation.org/knowledge-center/Documents/Changing-the-Principal-Supervisor-Role.pdf

Grissom, J. A., & Bartanen, B. (2019). Principal effectiveness and principal turnover. *Education Finance and Policy, 14*(3), 355–82. https://doi.org/10.1162/edfp_a_00256

Grissom, J. A., Egalite, A. J., & Lindsay, C. A. (2021). *How principals affect students and schools: A systematic synthesis of two decades of research.* The Wallace Foundation. Retrieved from http://www.wallacefoundation.org/principalsynthesis

Huang, T., Hochbein, C. & Simons, J. (2018). The relationship among school contexts, principal time use, school climate, and student achievement. *Educational Management, Administration & Leadership, 48*(2), 305–23.

Husain, A., Miller, L., & Player, D. (2021). Principal turnover: Using teacher-assessments of principal quality to understand who leaves the principalship. *Education Administration Quarterly, 57*(5), 683–715.

Leithwood, K., Louis, K. S., Anderson, S., & Wahlstrom, K. (2004). How leadership influences student learning. *Review of Research.* The Wallace Foundation. Retrieved from https://www.wallacefoundation.org/knowledge-center/pages/how-leadership-influences-student-learning.aspx

Loeb, S., Kalogrides, D., & Horng, E. L. (2010). Principal preferences and the uneven distribution of principals across schools. *Educational Evaluation and Policy Analysis, 32*(2), 205–29. https://doi.org/10.3102/0162373710369833

Marks, H. M., & Printy, S. M. (2003). Principal leadership and school performance: An integration of transformational and instructional leadership. *Educational Administration Quarterly, 39*(3), 370–97.

National Association of Secondary School Principals. (December 8, 2021). *NASSP survey signals a looming mass exodus of principals from schools.* NASSP. Retrieved from https://www.nassp.org/news/nassp-survey-signals-a-looming-mass-exodus-of-principals-from-schools/

Superville, D. (2019). *Principal turnover is a problem: New data could help districts combat it.* School & District Management. *Ed Week.* Retrieved from https://www.edweek.org/leadership/principal-turnover-is-a-problem-new-data-could-help-districts-combat-it/2019/12

Tekleselassie, A. A., & Choi, J. (2019). Understanding school principal attrition and mobility through hierarchical generalized linear modeling. *Educational Policy*. Advance online publication. Retrieved from https://doi.org/10.1177/0895904819857825

Thessin, R. (2019). Establishing productive principal/principal supervisor partnerships for instructional leadership. *Journal of Educational Administration*, *57*(5): 463–83.

About the Editor and Contributors

Kevin Badgett is associate professor and department chair for educational leadership in the College of Education at the University of Texas Permian Basin (UTPB). In addition to his experience at UTPB, Dr. Badgett has served in various roles in the K–12 setting as a teacher, school counselor, and as a campus and district level administrator. His research interests include school-community relations, leadership effectiveness, and teacher retention.

Rachel Biritz is PhD student, research assistant, and university supervisor in the Department of Educational and Organizational Leadership Development at Clemson University. She has served in teacher and leadership positions in the San Diego Unified School District, California, and Greenville County Schools, South Carolina. Her interests include using research to influence policy and leadership preparation programs.

Larry G. Daniel is dean and professor in the College of Education at the University of Texas Permian Basin. His forty-plus year career in education includes service as a middle/high school educator, an education professor, and a higher education leader. His areas of scholarly interest include educational leadership, teacher education, educational policy, and quantitative research methods.

Brennan Davis is assistant professor of education at Columbia College, where she teaches literacy, writing, and English education courses. Dr. Davis holds a PhD in language and literacy from the University of South Carolina and maintains research interests in two primary areas: effective professional development tools and processes for addressing issues of diversity in schools, particularly with veteran teachers, and innovative support systems for preservice and beginning teachers.

Gail Gilmore is new assistant professor of education leadership in the Zucker Family School of Education at The Citadel in Charleston, South Carolina. She has taught graduate courses in three other universities and previously served as a school superintendent.

Renée N. Jefferson teaches data collection and analysis and supervises action research projects conducted by graduate students in educational leadership, counselor education, and teacher education. Currently, Dr. Jefferson is a professor in the Zucker Family School of Education at The Citadel in Charleston, South Carolina.

Myron B. Labat is associate professor in the Department of Educational Leadership at Mississippi State University. His areas of research center on school and organizational culture and leadership theory. He has published his research in several peer reviewed publications and presented at state, regional, and national conferences. Prior to his work in the academy, Dr. Labat spent fourteen years in P–12 education as professional counselor and administrator.

Christine LeBlanc is assistant professor of education at Columbia College, where she teaches courses in early childhood, literacy, divergent learning, and school administration. She has more than thirty years of educational and administrative experience and multiple advanced degrees from the University of South Carolina, including a PhD in education administration. Her research interests include experiential learning, professional learning communities, and cultivating teacher leadership.

Leigh A. McMullan is assistant clinical professor in the Department of Educational Leadership at Mississippi State University. She has over twenty-five years in public education. Before joining the ranks of academia, Dr. McMullan served as a building-level administrator, school counselor, secondary science teacher, and middle science teacher. Dr. McMullan is a Framework for Understanding Poverty and Emotional Poverty certified trainer.

Kent Murray serves as professor in the educational leadership division of the Zucker Family School of Education at The Citadel in Charleston, South Carolina. He has served as a principal, school board member, and professor.

He has served in education for over thirty years, and he specializes in school law and finance.

Amanda Stefanski is assistant professor of special education at Columbia College, where she teaches courses related to education, special education, and trauma-informed instruction. Dr. Stefanski holds a PhD in curriculum and instruction from the University of Maryland and maintains research interests grounded in equity and inclusion, specifically in terms of teacher preparation for diverse student needs.

Paula Tharp is assistant professor in the Department of Educational Leadership at Mississippi State University. Paula's research and school system partnerships focus on practices for increasing capacity for improvement with a particular interest in supporting principals in high poverty rural school systems. Paula has served as a classroom teacher and administrator in Mississippi as well as a data specialist and a school improvement specialist across multiple states.

Lee Westberry is assistant professor of educational leadership in the Zucker Family School of Education at The Citadel Military College in Charleston, South Carolina. She also serves as the program coordinator for the division of ed leadership and the director of program development and enhancement for the ZFSOE. She provides principal professional development across the state and has recently published a new book titled *Putting the Pieces Together: A Systems Approach to School Leadership, The Final Piece: A Systems Approach to School Leadership* as well as *The Virtual Principal: The Many Facets of the Demanding Job*. Primary research interests include principal leadership, systems, and professional development.